AFGHANISTAN WAR

AMERICA AT WAR

Revolutionary War, Revised Edition
War of 1812, Revised Edition
U.S.-Mexican War, Revised Edition
Civil War, Revised Edition
Plains Indian Wars, Revised Edition
Spanish-American War, Revised Edition
World War I, Revised Edition
World War II, Revised Edition
Korean War, Revised Edition
Vietnam War, Revised Edition
Persian Gulf War, Revised Edition
Afghanistan War
Iraq War, Revised Edition
Chronology of Wars, Revised Edition

AFGHANISTAN WAR

RODNEY P. CARLISLE

JOHN S. BOWMAN
general editor

CHELSEA HOUSE
PUBLISHERS
An imprint of Infobase Publishing

Afghanistan War

Copyright © 2010 by Rodney P. Carlisle

Chelsea House
An imprint of Infobase Publishing
132 West 31st Street
New York NY 10001

Library of Congress Cataloging-in-Publication Data

Carlisle, Rodney P.
Afghanistan War / Rodney P. Carlisle, John S. Bowman, general editor.—1st ed.
p. cm.
Includes bibliographical references and index.
ISBN 978-0-8160-8119-6 (hc : alk. paper) 1. Afghan War, 2001—Juvenile literature.
I. Bowman, John S. II. Title.
DS371.412.C375 2010
958.104'7—dc22   2009048068

Chelsea House books are available at special discounts when purchased in bulk quantities for businesses, associations, institutions, or sales promotions. Please call our Special Sales Department in New York at (212) 967-8800 or (800) 322-8755.

You can find Chelsea House on the World Wide Web at http://www.chelseahouse.com

Text design by Erika K. Arroyo
Cover design by Takeshi Takahashi
Composition by Hermitage Publishing Services
Cover printed by Bang Printing, Brainerd, Minn.
Book printed and bound by Bang Printing, Brainerd, Minn.
Date printed: September 2010
Printed in the United States of America

10 9 8 7 6 5 4 3 2 1

This book is printed on acid-free paper.

All Web addresses were checked and verified to be correct at the time of publication. Because of the dynamic nature of the Web, some addresses and links may have changed since publication and may no longer be valid.

Contents

Preface

Immediately after the attacks by terrorists on September 11, 2001, on the World Trade Center in New York City and on the Pentagon in Washington, D.C., President George W. Bush demanded that the Afghan government arrest and turn over the organizers of the attacks, which killed nearly 3,000 civilians, the worst terrorist attack ever on American soil. Intelligence sources revealed that Osama bin Laden and his Islamic terrorist organization known as al-Qaeda planned and carried out the attacks.

The al-Qaeda organization provided funds to the government of Afghanistan. In turn, that government provided a safe haven for al-Qaeda. The Taliban dominated the Afghan government at that time. The Taliban movement based its philosophy of rule on a unique and distorted view of the Islamic religion and ran an extremely severe regime. Human rights were suppressed, and women, especially, were oppressed. The Taliban included some of the mujahideen that resisted the occupation of Afghanistan by the Soviet Union from 1979 to 1989.

When President Bush demanded the arrest of Osama bin Laden and other members of his organization, the Taliban government of Afghanistan refused to help and continued to protect bin Laden. In response, President Bush ordered units of the U.S. military to attack the Afghan government. The armed forces also tried to track down and bring to justice the perpetrators of the 9/11 attacks.

The Northern Alliance, an anti-Taliban Afghan military force, operated in the northern section of the country. They joined in the U.S. attack on the Taliban and soon succeeded in driving them from Kabul, the capital.

Meanwhile, U.S. forces captured air bases in the south and west of the country and soon began hot pursuit of Osama bin Laden, al-Qaeda members, and remnants of the Taliban regime. At first, the al-Qaeda leadership took refuge in caves and hiding places in the rugged eastern section of the country that bordered on Pakistan.

European countries that were members of the North Atlantic Treaty Organization (NATO) provided military assistance. NATO is an alliance of nations organized under the North Atlantic Treaty to promote collective defense. The al-Qaeda attacks on the United States were the first attacks in the treaty's 60-year history that led to the creation of a NATO-based military unit. Some 20 nations participated by providing military aid to the U.S.-led attack on the Taliban regime. By December 9, 2001, the Taliban was routed.

In December 2001, the Afghan Transitional Administration was set up, and Hamid Karzai was named chairman. Meanwhile, U.S. troops pursued Osama bin Laden into the caves of eastern Afghanistan. Within months, however, the al-Qaeda leaders quietly left, taking refuge over the international border in Pakistan.

The al-Qaeda leaders moved into a section of Pakistan called the North-West Frontier Province. This province is run by many small fiefdoms and was inundated by Afghan refugees in the 1980s. Many of the Taliban came from these areas, and the Taliban organization remains very strong in North-West Frontier, making it easy for Osama bin Laden and other members of al-Qaeda to find refuge in the area's numerous small villages.

Within Afghanistan, it soon became apparent that the remaining Taliban and other local military groups headed by independent warlords resisted the establishment of a central government in Kabul. Thus, even though the war that overthrew the Taliban regime ended, military attacks on the government, on NATO forces, and on U.S. troops continued.

The United States then became involved in a much larger war in Iraq. In 2003, U.S. and allied forces overthrew the Iraqi dictatorial regime of Saddam Hussein. As U.S. troops occupied that country with a number of partners, including most notably Great Britain, the pitched battles of that war were also over quickly. However, Hussein loyalists and al-Qaeda–funded terrorists continued to kill American and other occupying troops. Suicide bombers and bombs placed at mosques, public markets, and police stations represented a continuing threat to peace. Improvised explosive devices (IEDs) made from artillery shells and other explosives continued to kill Americans in trucks and Humvees.

As American casualties in Iraq mounted, they reached more than 4,350 fatalities by the end of 2009. Because of this tragic count, American public attention remained more focused on the terrible events in Iraq than on the low-key conflict in Afghanistan. By the time of the U.S. elections in 2008, it seemed a somewhat stable regime had emerged in Iraq. In late 2008, the Iraqi government approved the U.S.-Iraq Status of Forces Agreement, establishing that U.S. combat forces would withdraw from Iraqi cities by June 30, 2009, and all U.S. forces would be out of Iraq by December 31, 2011, subject to further negotiations.

Barack Obama won election to the U.S. presidency in November 2008 and committed to withdrawing U.S. forces from Iraq. He also committed to making a stronger effort to bring peace to Afghanistan. However, the situation in Afghanistan remained extremely difficult and might not be solved by adding more troops. Several deep-seated issues made it seem unlikely that peace in Afghanistan could be achieved quickly. Although Hamid Karzai remained nominally in charge of the government, some people regarded him as little more than the mayor of Kabul, rather than president of the whole nation. Real power continued to rest with local leaders. Although Karzai belonged to the majority Pashtun ethnic group, much of the low-level administrative staff in the central government came from the Uzbek and Tajik ethnic groups of the northern regions, a fact resented by the majority Pashtuns.

Even more serious problems plagued the country. Almost half of the money from exports came from the illegal trade in opium. In fact, it has been estimated that more than 90 percent of the world's heroin supply is derived from opium grown in Afghanistan. Although the Afghan farmers who grow the opium receive a small proportion of the illegal money, most of the cash goes to middlemen and traders. These criminals regularly bribe border guards, police, and other officials to prevent being arrested. Thus, criminal corruption based on the narcotics trade is widespread. Afghanistan is rated as one of the most corrupt countries in the world.

Meanwhile, the Taliban in the North-West Frontier Province of Pakistan continue to help Afghan guerrillas. They provided training, weapons, money, and safe havens for fighters against the government in Kabul. The same resources are used against NATO and U.S. troops trying to maintain order and against soldiers trying to set up basic services such as electric power, schools, clinics, and hospitals. Afghanistan remains one of the poorest countries in the world.

Afghanistan suffers from high illiteracy rates. The country is extremely poor. There is no stable rule of law. Most Afghans hold extremely conservative religious positions. All of these factors contribute to its difficulty in developing a stable regime. Many observers doubt whether a democratic style of government such as that in the United States or western Europe could emerge in Afghanistan.

As Americans faced the continuing problems brought on by the war in Afghanistan, they have argued over a great many issues arising out of the war and its long and bloody aftermath. Among the issues considered in this book are the following:

1. What are the historical roots of the issues dividing Afghanistan and making it so difficult to govern?
2. To what extent did American support for the anti-Soviet mujahideen in the 1980s contribute to the later rise to power of the Taliban?
3. What was the nature of the Taliban regime, and how did it suppress civil liberties and the rights of women?
4. Was the United States justified in going to war against the Taliban regime in Afghanistan after the terrorist attacks of 9/11?
5. How did Osama bin Laden and other senior al-Qaeda leaders evade being captured by American forces?
6. What are the exact sources of the continuing guerrilla attacks against the government of Afghanistan and the American and NATO troops there?
7. Why has the regime of Hamid Karzai been unable to establish control of the country?
8. What role in the continuing struggle in Afghanistan has been played by Taliban forces based in the North-West Frontier Province of Pakistan?
9. What is the proper way for the United States to treat captured members of al-Qaeda?
10. To what extent has the American effort to bring peace and democracy to Iraq prevented a solution to the problems of Afghanistan in the period from 2003 to 2009?

These and other issues about the war cannot be answered with a simple, one-sentence statement. Informed and intelligent discussion about these deeply controversial issues is possible, as long as those involved in the discussion look at the facts and base their discussion on information, not on emotional outrage. Even after close study of the facts, however, it is likely that Americans will continue to disagree about the sorts of policies that should be adopted.

It is in the nature of American democracy and American politics to disagree about policy. Those arguments are most likely to produce decent solutions when the discussion takes into account the facts. In this work, every attempt has been made to present the facts in an objective and balanced way, in order to help students discuss the issues in a reasonable fashion.

The book is organized in 14 chapters, starting with a chapter that brings the war in Afghanistan to its immediate level with an episode in the life of American troops on the ground. Each chapter contains at least one boxed topic that explores related issues in greater depth and that can be read separately from the chapter. Illustrations—many of them in full color—and maps provide ways to visualize what has been going on in Afghanistan. The work also provides definitions, dates, and descriptions of groups and events in straightforward language. A glossary of terms at the end of the book provides definitions of the unfamiliar terminology used. A final section lists sources for further information, including books and Web sites.

IN ACTION, AFGHANISTAN

It was midwinter in Afghanistan as the U.S. Marines inside Bone-crusher inched down a highway in the middle of Taliban country in Farah Province. They were leading a convoy down the dusty two-lane highway that connected the towns of Delaram and Bakwa. They had just passed a stalled truck that had unwisely pulled out of the convoy and then struck a bomb. The blast came from an improvised explosive device (IED).

Sergeant Mario Spencer and his men stayed in their machine, a Buffalo mine protected clearance vehicle (MPCV), a 13-foot-high special purpose truck that was featured in the movie *Transformers*. In fact, Spencer and his four-man team had named their MPCV "Bonecrusher" after one of the transforming robots in that movie. Another MPCV that carried the unit's commanding officer was dubbed "Megatron."

In early February 2009, the *Wall Street Journal* published an account of the team's work, written by the journalist Yochi Dreazon. The story described both the mission of Spencer and his team and the equipment they used. The information about the MPCV was news for most Americans, who knew few details of the way the war in Afghanistan was being fought.

Inside the truck, the men were protected by three-inch-thick window glass. On the front of the vehicle, a 30-foot robotic arm could be folded back or extended out, with its protected cameras and a blade/shovel to dig out IEDs. The bottom of the vehicle was V-shaped, so it could better withstand explosions. Inside the protected cabin, the men would hook up their iPods to speakers and fill the hull with the sounds of Jimi Hendrix.

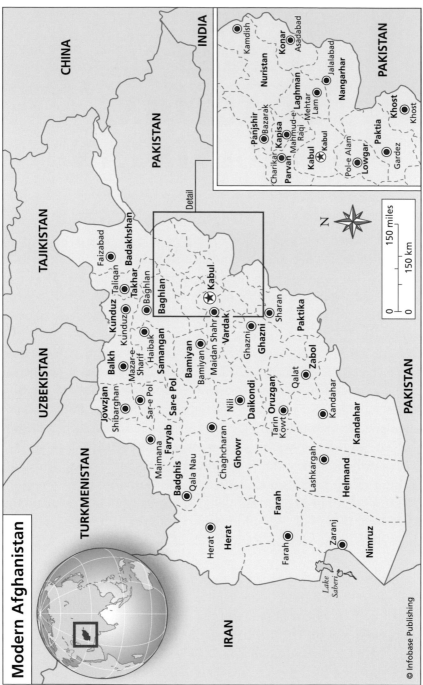

Modern Afghanistan

© Infobase Publishing

The road from Delaram to Bakwa was dangerous. The enemy would plant IEDs, often artillery shells wired to go off when vehicles passed over. Some of the IEDs were simply jugs of explosives wired to pressure-sensitive triggers in the road. Officials have estimated that IEDs killed about 2,000 American soldiers in Iraq and Afghanistan by 2009.

As the MPCV inched down the highway at 8 A.M., word came of a suspicious spot next to the side of the road. Freshly turned dirt hinted that someone had planted something very dangerous there.

Bonecrusher pulled up next to the spot. Inside, Corporal Tom Ruggles handled the small yellow control pad. Working the paddles and toggle switches, he extended the robot arm and dug a rectangle around the suspicious spot. Sure enough, a line of black wiring showed up in the dirt, indicating a roadway trigger.

Working the arm, Ruggles soon dug a blue plastic jug out of the dirt. He lifted it out and planned to drop it far from the road where it could be harmlessly set off. But the bomb stuck on the claw at the end of the arm. There was no choice. Ruggles and a teammate got out of Bonecrusher and began wrestling the bomb loose by hand. It was 15 minutes before they were able to free it and set it down.

The Buffalo MPCV is designed to counter IEDs by safely detecting and inspecting them. *(Department of Defense)*

THE BUFFALO MINE PROTECTED CLEARANCE VEHICLE

Designed to safely navigate and clear mines in dangerous combat zones, the Buffalo was built in response to the terrible toll that IEDs were taking on lighter, less protected vehicles like the Humvee (high mobility multipurpose wheeled vehicle; HMMWV). It is a medium-sized totally enclosed trucklike vehicle. Its body has extremely heavy armor plate, and it has a V-shaped undercarriage to deflect the force of any explosion away from the vehicle. In front is a large, articulated, movable arm designed to search for IEDs and other dangerous ordnance.

Specifications
Seats: six
Tires: 52 inches, rated for 55 miles per hour (MPH)
Horsepower: 400
Windows: three-inch-thick glass
Height: 13 feet
Length: 27 feet
Cost: about $1 million
Weight: 45,320 lbs; gross weight with fuel and equipment: 80,000 lbs
Rear access door
V-shaped under hull to deflect blast

A bomb disposal team came and examined the IED. It had enough explosive to completely demolish a Humvee, even one that was armored. Most probably, if it had gone off next to a Humvee, it would have killed the crew.

The disposal team took the jug out into the open desert where they wired a small charge of their own to it. At the countdown, it blasted a harmless hole in the gravel and dirt. Watching from Bonecrusher, Spencer and Ruggles felt some satisfaction. Then they started down the road again.

Spencer had joined the marines nine years earlier. Like many in the services, he came from a family that had provided more than one generation to the military. His father had served in the U.S. Coast Guard, and his example had inspired Mario. Spencer married Rafaelina Anderson, a fellow marine, and they had two children. Corporal

Jason Mueske, who worked alongside Spencer in the MPCV, was also a second-generation marine. His father, Allen Mueske, had served almost four years in Vietnam.

Spencer and Ruggles's MPCV was one of a number of special-purpose heavy-duty vehicles made by Force Protection, Inc., a company based in South Carolina. After years of experience in both Iraq and Afghanistan, the U.S. Marine Corps and the U.S. Army had learned a lot. Humvees, although they looked tough, were no match for roadside IEDs.

When the troops began scrounging scrap metal and welding their own protective armor onto Humvees, the American public was outraged. Why was it impossible for the United States, with its high-tech capabilities and industrial base, to provide decent and safe transportation to the troops fighting in those two countries?

IMPROVISED EXPLOSIVE DEVICES

An IED can be any type of homemade device designed to cause injury or death. Some contain only explosives, while others are made with poisonous chemicals or radioactive material. There are many different types, sizes, and ways of delivering them. Some use surplus military explosives, such as artillery shells, while others are made from homemade explosives packed in a box or plastic jug. A wide variety of methods of setting them off have been employed.

In areas with cell phone service, as in Iraq, it was common to find IEDs set to go off with a phone call to a cell phone wired to a switch and detonator in the IED. The terrorist would wait in ambush and punch in all but the last number of the detonator phone on his own cell phone. Then as a target vehicle neared, he would send the last number, hoping to time the explosion as the Humvee or truck passed over the bomb.

Some IEDs would be mounted on utility or telephone poles, just at the right height to kill or injure a tank commander standing up and looking out of his tank or a driver in a truck.

In Afghanistan, IEDs are often buried next to the road in a pile of trash or scrap lumber or in a shallow hole. Some are wired to a pressure-sensitive trigger embedded in the road surface. Others are left in abandoned or wrecked vehicles. To clear a road requires investigation of every suspicious pile of rags or junk by the side of the road, a very slow process.

This U.S. Marine convoy of armored Humvees is traveling through Helmand Province in southern Afghanistan on a mission to combat Taliban forces in the area. *(Department of Defense)*

Among the responses was the Buffalo, along with other strengthened vehicles. Another in the family of mine resistant ambush protected (MRAP) vehicles was the six-wheeled Cougar. That tough machine could carry a squad of 12 soldiers or four explosive ordnance disposal experts with their own small robot that could be wheeled out to examine bombs and IEDs.

Like the Buffalo, the Cougar had heavy armor and thickened glass, but it stood a little shorter, at 104 inches (just under nine feet). On a good road, its tires could allow it to run at 55 MPH, even faster for shorter sprints.

INTERNATIONAL SECURITY ASSISTANCE FORCE

The International Security Assistance Force (ISAF) grew from a small group of nations from the North Atlantic Treaty Organization (NATO) to include many others outside the organization, such as Hungary and Slovenia. By 2009, 41 countries provided troops and equipment, bringing the total number of foreign troops in the country to about 72,000.

By October 2009, the American contingent was about 34,800; while some other countries provided significant large groups:

Australia	1,350
Canada	2,830
France	3,095
Germany	4,365
Italy	2,795
Netherlands	2,160
Poland	1,910
United Kingdom	9,000

Due to troop rotations and changing commitments, numbers can vary. These figures are only approximate.

At first, ISAF forces concentrated on helping to maintain order in the capital city of Kabul. In 2004, ISAF forces helped to police and maintain order in some of the northern provinces of Afghanistan. In 2005, they took on security in the western provinces. In 2006, ISAF took charge of operations in the southern provinces. Later in 2006, U.S. troops in the eastern provinces became part of the integrated ISAF command system.

The international troops helped in training Afghan troops. They also helped build schools, clinics, and other needed facilities, as well as mounting patrols against guerrilla bands and terrorists.

In each province, commanders from one of the nations have the lead or command responsibility. The United States retained the lead command in the southern provinces around Kabul, where the Taliban guerrillas were most active.

These new machines were only part of the American military response to the war in Afghanistan. Of course, technology alone could not solve the deep problems there or bring peace to the country.

Peace in Afghanistan would require that the young Americans who put their lives on the line worked under good and informed leadership. Pushing a convoy of trucks safely through remote provinces to supply bases was one small element in the much larger struggle to get some law and order established.

Troops from the United States, Britain, Germany, and other European allies had been fighting in Afghanistan since 2001. This coalition of troops was organized into a group called the International Security Assistance Force (ISAF). The Taliban regime that ruled Afghanistan soon collapsed, driven from power by a combination of Afghan resistance armies and ISAF soldiers. However, although the quick war seemed over in weeks, peace did not follow the military defeat of the Taliban.

As in Iraq, sporadic ambushes, roadside bombings, and disruptive raids raged. Elements of the Taliban in armed bands struck against the new Afghan government, against foreign aid agencies, and especially against U.S. and European troops who tried to bring stability.

Young men and women in the United States, many of them fresh from high school, volunteered for the army, navy, marines, and air force and risked their lives in warfare, as had generations of Americans before them. Their families were proud, but they also dreaded that word might come of injury, sickness, or death in the long battle to establish a free country in Afghanistan.

The young soldiers and their families, as did their leaders, wanted to understand the distant country and its war. This book is written to tell the story of that distant war.

AFGHANISTAN'S HISTORY

A look at a map of Asia shows that Afghanistan lies among some of the world's largest and most powerful countries. To the north lie the countries that made up both the former Russian Empire and the former Soviet Union. To the south and east lie Pakistan and India. (The British ruled India, which included Pakistan, as part of the British Empire from 1858–1947.

To the west of Afghanistan lies Iran, formerly Persia. And at its northeast tip, Afghanistan shares a short stretch of border with China. Today, China and India each have more than 1 billion people, and Pakistan and Russia each have more than 140 million; neighboring Iran has more than 60 million people, while Afghanistan has only 31 million.

Because of its location on the trade routes from west to east and north to south, Afghanistan served for centuries as a crossroad for major European and Asian civilizations. Foreign armies invaded and fought over Afghanistan for more than 2,000 years. Despite its powerful neighbors and many invasions, only rarely have the invaders been able to control the country for very long. Its rugged terrain; its variety of local ethnic, linguistic, and tribal groups; and its warrior heritage have all made the country very hard to govern. The ancient Persians ruled over Afghanistan in the sixth century B.C.E. Alexander the Great used the country as a path to India in 330 B.C.E.

The Mongol conqueror Genghis Khan held Afghanistan in the 13th century, and a century later, Tamerlane ruled over Afghanistan. In the 16th century, a descendant of Tamerlane set up the Mughal Empire, with the capital in Kabul, the city that is the modern capital of the country. That empire comprised most of the Indian subcontinent as well. In the 17th century, Persians ruled Afghanistan.

This rather fanciful 18th-century engraving depicts Genghis Khan, whose Mongol forces overran Afghanistan, ca. 1220. *(The Stapleton Collection/ Art Resource, N.Y.)*

In 1747, Afghanistan became an independent state under the Pashtun leader Ahmad Shah Durrani. Durrani's empire lasted for almost 100 years, controlling parts of what are now Iran and Pakistan as well. For generations, his descendants have remained powerful local leaders.

The British had a vast empire with huge colonies in Africa and Asia, but they failed to take over Afghanistan in the 19th century. The British fought two Afghan Wars (1839–42 and 1878–80). Although the most powerful country in the world at the time, Britain could only establish influence, not control, in Afghanistan. Britain hoped to prevent Russia from taking over the area and wanted to protect their own dominance of India.

Some cynical writers called the struggle for influence and control between the Russian Empire and the British Empire in the mountains of Afghanistan "The Great Game." Neither side ever won the game.

Timur the Lame, known in the West as Tamerlane (1363–1405), was a Mongol leader whose empire included most of Afghanistan. He is depicted here dealing with a Persian ruler. *(HIP/Art Resource, N.Y.)*

In 1919, Afghanistan became a truly independent country, ruled by its own king and recognized internationally as a separate nation. Other countries recognized Afghanistan as independent under the Treaty of

Pilgrims from Afghanistan arrive at Kandahar Army Airfield, preparing to fly to Mecca while making the hajj, the pilgrimage that is one of the principal religious obligations of Muslims. *(Department of Defense)*

Rawalpindi in that same year. The first king, Amanullah, pledged the country would stay neutral.

Even though an independent country, Afghanistan still remained a hot spot because of its location. After 1919, it lay between the British Empire in India to the south and east and the Soviet Union that had replaced the Russian Empire to the north. And, as in the past, rebels kept up the tradition of fighting under local leaders and warlords. Rebels still took refuge in the mountains in small bands, keeping the country torn up with war and military uprisings.

The ethnic and tribal divisions in Afghanistan all contributed to the difficulty in governing the country as a unified nation. Divisions between the different branches of Islam, the Sunni and Shia, added a religious element to the conflicts within Afghanistan.

Muhammad Nadir Shah became king of Afghanistan in 1929 with British diplomatic support. He tried to begin some reforms to modernize the country, but assassins killed him in 1933. His reforms had angered traditional Muslims and Muslim religious leaders.

From 1933 to 1973, his son, Muhammad Zahir Shah, ruled the country. Zahir Shah also tried to modernize the country, but he wisely decided to do so in a gradual way. His government built many schools and sent many Afghans to foreign countries to get educated. Trained teachers, technicians, and army officers returned with ideas and knowledge gained in Europe, America, and the Soviet Union.

General Muhammad Daoud Khan, Zahir Shah's brother-in-law, served as prime minister in the 1950s. Daoud ran the country like a dictatorship, and opponents finally forced him to resign in 1963. A famine swept through Afghanistan in 1972, and Daoud, with support from the Soviet Union, overthrew the monarchy in 1973. The king

ISLAM

Islam is a religion practiced in many countries around the world. It is based on the teachings of the prophet Muhammad (570–632 C.E.) who lived in what is now the modern kingdom of Saudi Arabia. Islam means "submission" as in "submission to the will of God." In Islam, God is known as Allah. Those who practice and believe in Islam are known as Muslims.

Muslims believe that Muhammad was the last of the prophets. Among earlier prophets recognized under Islam are Abraham, Moses, David, and Jesus.

The revelations to Muhammad are collected in a holy book known as the Quran (often transliterated as Koran). The revelations are organized in order of length, from the shortest to the longest. Personal sayings and teachings of Muhammad, together with accounts of his actions and his decisions, are collected in a separate volume, known as the Hadith. Islam draws on both the Quran and the Hadith.

Although there are numerous sects of Islam, the two major divisions are the Sunni and the Shia (also known as Shiite). Shia tend to believe that all government should be empowered by religious leaders. The Sunni usually accept the idea of a civil government separated from religion. The Sunni and Shia also disagree about the line of descent from the prophet Muhammad and his family.

The majority of the population in the modern country of Iran is Shia, and Shia groups are found in other countries as well. In Iraq, under Saddam Hussein, most power rested with the minority Arab Sunni population, who tended to suppress the rights of the Shia majority. In Afghanistan, most of the population are Sunni. One ethnic group in Afghanistan, the Hazaras, however, are mostly Shia.

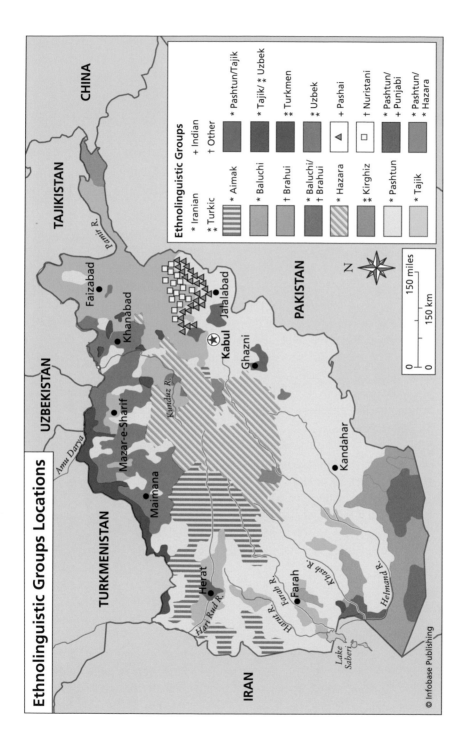

Ethnolinguistic Groups Locations

Ethnolinguistic Groups

* Iranian   + Indian
* Turkic   † Other

* Aimak
* Baluchi
† Brahui
* Baluchi/ † Brahui
* Hazara
* Kirghiz
* Pashtun
* Tajik

* Pashtun/Tajik
* Tajik/ ** Uzbek
** Turkmen
** Uzbek
+ Pashai
† Nuristani
* Pashtun/ + Punjabi
* Pashtun/ * Hazara

© Infobase Publishing

AFGHAN ETHNIC GROUPS

Exact proportions of the various ethnic groups making up Afghanistan are difficult to state precisely. A 1990s study showed the following.

Pashtun	40 percent
Tajiks	25+ percent
Hazaras	18 percent
Uzbeks	6+ percent
Turkmen	2+ percent
Other groups	8+ percent

The Pashtun (Pushtun or Pakhtun) are made up of 11 different tribes. In addition to the estimated 10 million living in Afghanistan, another 14 million Pashtun people live in Pakistan. In Afghanistan, the Pashtun heartland runs in a large crescent-shaped belt following the Afghan-Pakistani border on the east. It then runs southward from Nuristan, across the south, and north along the Iranian border almost to the city of Herat. Small isolated groups of Pashtun live throughout the nation, settled among other ethnic groups.

The Pashtun speak several dialects of Pashtu; one Pashtu speaker can understand another speaking a different dialect. The language is related to the Persian spoken in Iran.

went into exile in Italy. Daoud then declared Afghanistan a republic and named it the Democratic Republic of Afghanistan.

During Daoud's regime, a Marxist political party along the lines of the Soviet Communist Party developed to resist Daoud. That party, the People's Democratic Party of Afghanistan (PDPA), had two different factions. The more radical branch demanded immediate change. The moderate branch wanted a more gradual approach. The radical branch called themselves the Khalq (masses), while the gradualist branch took the name Parcham (banner).

Daoud had both branches of the party outlawed and their leaders imprisoned. Daoud tried to reduce the dependence of his government on the powerful Soviet neighbor. But a coup by the army in 1978 overthrew Daoud, and he and his family were assassinated.

The coup leaders called their fight the Great Saur Revolution, after *Saur*, the word for April, the month of the rebellion. The Saur Revolution was not a widespread revolution. Rather, the leaders simply arrested a few government officials, made sure they controlled the military, and took over the capital city.

The army leaders put the leader of the Khalq branch of the PDPA, Nur Muhammad Taraki, in power. He served as president of a revolutionary council. Taraki's new government signed a treaty with the Soviet Union. Taraki tried to begin a series of deep reforms, including breaking up large landholdings and limiting the power of the Muslim clergy. Taraki did not imprison or kill his PDPA opponents in the Parcham branch of the party, but he exiled some of them by giving them jobs as ambassadors in faraway countries.

Taraki's Khalq government faced widespread uprisings led by conservative Muslims. Refugees fled into neighboring Pakistan. Faced with these troubles, the Khalq regime grew weaker. The Soviets did not entirely trust Taraki and his radical faction. Taraki asked the Soviet government to send military aid and troops to help his government put down the uprisings, but the Soviets resisted the idea and provided only limited help such as advisers and matériel.

After an internal power struggle, Prime Minister Hafizullah Amin kicked out Taraki in September 1979. Amin had Taraki killed and took power as president. The Soviets suspected Amin was going to work with the United States because he had been educated in the United States. Amin did not last very long, because in December 1979, Soviet troops assisted in another coup that threw out Amin's government.

Amin was killed in the battle to take over the presidential palace. Rumors persisted that the Soviets had ordered his killing. The exiled leader of the Parcham faction of the PDPA, Babrak Karmal, returned from his job as ambassador to Czechoslovakia, and with Soviet support Karmal was installed "to save the revolution" in Afghanistan. That is what Soviet paratroopers told the staff of Radio Kabul when they took it over on the night of the coup.

Outside observers tried to understand developments in Afghanistan. The two branches of the PDPA acted like competing parties. Moscow controlled neither one of the parties, unlike how the Soviets controlled other Communist regimes around the world. Also, it seemed strange that Babrak Karmal of the moderate Parcham group got more Soviet support than Taraki and Amin, who had led the radical faction.

As the Parcham coup took place, about 40,000 Soviet troops invaded the country. Some observers thought that the Soviet Union had helped organize the coup that put Karmal in power. Others concluded that the fight between the PDPA factions went on without outside interference. However, Karmal willingly accepted Soviet aid. After he took power, Soviet forces continued to flow into the country. They supported the Karmal regime and tried to help him bring about reforms.

Both the United States and the UN General Assembly condemned the Soviet invasion. The number of Soviet troops soon climbed to more than 120,000 as the Soviets tried to maintain order against growing Afghan resistance. A number of independent small armies and bands of fighters made up the resistance against Soviet forces. The resistance fighters were called mujahideen, or "holy warriors." Not all of the mujahideen wanted to establish a strict Muslim state, but some of them did.

As many as seven distinct tribal, ideological, or warlord units made up the mujahideen that had bases and support in Pakistan. At least another four groups received support from Iran. The various groups did not have a single central leadership. The U.S. Central Intelligence Agency (CIA) routed weapons and financial support to the mujahideen through Pakistan.

The Inter-Services Intelligence (ISI), the largest intelligence service in Pakistan, managed the distribution of money and weapons and trained fighters. The ISI tended to favor the more religiously committed units of the mujahideen.

The Soviet forces, like the British and other invaders before them, could not control the country. The Soviet army had not been trained to fight against irregular guerrilla bands like those of the mujahideen. Furthermore, the Soviet army faced more than the traditional difficulties that had defeated all previous invaders of Afghanistan. The United States provided the mujahideen with modern weapons that could shoot down Soviet helicopters. Also, Soviet armored cars and tanks did not work very well in the rugged mountain terrain. The Soviets relied on heavy guns, more useful in attacks on a heavily equipped army. The Soviet artillery showed up poorly against individual mujahideen fighters equipped with hand-carried weapons.

To make matters worse, tens of thousands of Soviet troops fell ill with diseases. The Soviet government admitted that the mujahideen killed at least 14,000 Soviet soldiers and civilians. Independent estimates put the real total much higher, closer to 30,000.

The long-drawn-out war in Afghanistan contributed to political crises inside the Soviet Union. By the late 1980s, the Soviet leader

MUJAHIDEEN PARTIES

During the mujahideen resistance to the Soviet Army and the PDPA government, at least 11 separate party organizations fought against the Soviets. Each had its own fighters, organized in as many as 170 small bands under a chief or warlord.

Islamic Party (HIH)—Hizb-i-Islami Gulbuddin. This party was established in 1974(?) as part of the resistance to the Daoud government. Later it split into two factions. The HIH received more help from the United States and Saudi Arabia than any other group. It later became a major ally of the Taliban.

Islamic Party (HIK)—Hizb-i-Islami Khalis. This wing was set up by Mawlawi Khalis and was more moderate than the HIH branch. Khalis recruited from government and religious schools and also drew lots of members from government army deserters.

Islamic Union for the Liberation of Afghanistan (IUA)—Ittihad-i-Islami. The IUA was founded by Abd Al-Rab Abdul-Rassul Sayyaf and heavily financed by the Saudi Wahhabi sect. It is said that Osama bin Laden arranged much of its funding personally.

Afghanistan National Liberation Front (ANLF)—Jebh-e-Nejat-i-Melli. This was a largely nonreligious, moderate party. The

Mikhail Gorbachev began planning a withdrawal. He hoped to compromise with the mujahideen.

Karmal left power in May 1986. The new leader of the PDPA in Afghanistan, Najibullah Ahmadzai, had previously headed the Afghan secret police. Najibullah brought in some non-Communist political leaders in hopes of creating a broader-based government. However, the fact that Najibullah was a Tajik ruling the country did not sit well with the larger Pashtun ethnic group.

Meanwhile, the Soviets withdrew. The last Soviet troops departed in February 1989. Najibullah continued to face a large military resistance to his regime from the mujahideen. They did not want to share power with a man they saw as a Soviet puppet.

After further infighting among the mujahideen, various groups in Pakistan chose one of the most moderate of their members, Sebqhatullah Mojadeddi, to act as president of the Afghan interim government in 1989. Mojadeddi ran a sort of government in exile from Pakistan.

ANLF leader Sebqhatullah Mojadeddi became president of the Afghan interim government from 1989 to 1992.

Islamic Revolutionary Movement (IRMA)—Harakat-e-Inqilab-i-Islami. The IRMA leadership included traditionalist religious leaders, and this organization provided some of the key leaders in the later Taliban movement.

Islamic Society (JIA)—Jamiat-i-Islami. JIA was established by the Tajik leader Burhanuddin Rabbani, who went into exile in Pakistan in 1974. This party was supported by two commanders in northern Afghanistan, Ahmad Shah Massoud and Ismail Khan, both with better organizations than other armies. Rabbani took over the Afghan government in 1992.

National Islamic Front of Afghanistan (NIFA)—Mahaz-e-Melli. This party favored the restoration of the former king Zahir Shah. NIFA recruited members from among the wealthy landholding families. Its primary power base came from seven specific tribes of Pashtun people.

Four smaller political parties worked out of Iran. They received far less aid than the Pakistan-based parties and operated mostly in the Hazara region of Afghanistan where the population follows the Shia branch of Islam, as do the Iranians.

Over the next three years, the mujahideen continued to fight against the Najibullah regime. By early 1991, foreign observers estimated that Najibullah controlled only about 10 percent of the country, mostly around Kabul, the capital, and a few other cities.

In 1992, the United States, Pakistan, and Russia stopped sending weapons. The central government could not renew its supplies of ammunition or guns, and Najibullah's government collapsed in April. Many government troops, sometimes whole units at a time, switched sides and went over to the mujahideen. The Tajik commander, Ahmad Shah Massoud, took over Kabul. Najibullah sought refuge in the UN compound in Kabul. Sebqhatullah Mojadeddi took power for two months, running a coalition government based on the various parties of the mujahideen.

Burhanuddin Rabbani, a Tajik, replaced Mojadeddi after two months. Rabbani's military support came from several moderate Islamic forces, including the army of Massoud. Most Pashtun, 40 percent of the Afghan people, believed that the government should

AFGHANISTAN CHRONOLOGY 1919–1992

1919
- Afghanistan established as an independent monarchy.

1929
- Muhammad Nadir Shah becomes king, leads reforms, with British support.

1933
- King Nadir Shah is assassinated.

1933–73
- King Muhammad Zahir Shah rules.

1977
- Muhammad Daoud Khan (prime minister under Zahir Shah) comes to power.

1978
- Muhammad Daoud is assassinated; army stages coup with Khalq leaders.

1979
- Amin stages palace coup and executes Taraki.

1979
- Soviet troops enter, begin occupation; Amin is killed, and the Parcham leader Babrak Karmal takes power with Soviet help.

1986
- Karmal is replaced by Najibullah Ahmadzai (former head of secret police).

1986–89
- United States provides aid to mujahideen against Soviets and Communist regime.

1989
- Soviets complete their withdrawal from Afghanistan.

1992
- Najibullah regime collapses under attacks from mujahideen.

be run by Pashtun people, not by the small minority Tajiks from the northern section of the country. Even so, Rabbani was supported by the strongest and most disciplined of the mujahideen armies, so efforts by Pashtun groups to remove him from power took several years.

An Afghan family from the Pashtun tribe, one of the dominant peoples in southern Afghanistan, sits together in their home in Kabul, the capital. *(Department of Defense)*

In 1994, while Rabbani still ruled in Kabul, dozens of petty chieftains and their bands roamed freely in the Pashtun southern and eastern provinces. The road from Kandahar to Pakistan, an old caravan route and later a truck route, fell into local chiefs' hands. They set up barricades on the road and would charge truck drivers a toll or bribe to pass through. The truck drivers of Kandahar were outraged as the lawless conditions ruined their businesses.

While not exactly anarchy, it was clear that the country had broken up into groups of provinces controlled by local leaders and warlords, with some provinces under the gangster rule of bands of roving gunmen.

The mujahideen leader Gulbuddin Hekmatyar controlled a small region to the south and east of Kabul. Another army, under Ismail Khan, had its base in Herat. In the north, the Uzbek warlord Rashid Dostum held six provinces. A sporadic civil war was taking place, especially as Hekmatyar made several attempts to throw out the Rabbani regime in Kabul.

The southeastern region around Kandahar had dozens of bandits and petty ex-mujahideen warlords who competed for control over small patches of territory. In 1994, Hekmatyar and Khan attacked

Kabul, but Massoud held out for a while and kept the capital in the hands of the Tajik-dominated regime of Rabbani.

Pashtuns in the south and east were outraged at Tajik control of the capital. Most people in the region were tired of years of warfare and disruption. Local leaders in the Pashtun southeast hoped for some solution. They were supported especially by the truck drivers of Kandahar who demanded that the bandits who blocked the highway be stopped.

The opening of that highway would eventually play a major role in the rise of the Taliban, which would, in turn, lead to the U.S. war in Afghanistan.

THE SOVIET
INVASION

1979–1989

Afghanistan is a unique country, suffering from extreme poverty. It has been difficult and sometimes impossible to govern. Many of its people are very conservative in their social and religious views. They have long resisted attempts by central governments to bring reform or progress. The languages spoken there are not widely studied in Europe, the United States, or Russia.

All of these facts have made it difficult for outsiders to understand how to deal with Afghanistan. In the period of 1979 to 1989, the Soviet Union attempted to control Afghanistan and demonstrated how hard it was to understand and bring peace to the country. The United States and others attempted to help the Afghans oppose the Soviets, which contributed to the Soviet difficulties. But the aid ended up helping people who hated the United States as much as they hated the Soviets.

When the Soviets invaded, they were upbeat because of recent political and military successes. Through the decade of the 1970s, international communism had won some tough fights. In 1975, U.S. forces had pulled out of South Vietnam, leaving North Vietnamese Communists in charge. Communist and pro-Soviet regimes ruled in Cambodia and Laos. In Africa, the countries of Angola, Mozambique, and Ethiopia all had regimes friendly to the Soviets.

In Latin America, both Nicaragua and El Salvador favored the Soviets. Soviet military specialists worked in Cuba, Vietnam, Angola, Congo, Egypt, and Syria. Soviet spies and Soviet-funded Communist Parties operated in Europe.

THE SOVIET DECISION

The Soviet decision to send troops to Afghanistan was made in secret. The political leaders of the Soviet Union, organized in the Politburo, made the decision. They went against the advice and objections of their army leaders. In Afghanistan, the leaders of the People's Democratic Party of Afghanistan (PDPA), both Hafizullah Amin and Nur Muhammad Taraki made repeated requests for the Soviets to come in to help them stabilize the country against the resistance to their regime.

The Soviet army estimated that it would take a huge contingent of forces to win in Afghanistan. But the civilians did not take their advice. In fact, the civilian leader, General Secretary Brezhnev, was influenced by the head of the KGB (the Soviet spy agency), Yuri Andropov. The army's own intelligence agency, the GRU, opposed the invasion of Afghanistan. Brezhnev made the final decision to send in the troops.

The Soviets relied on KGB information rather than GRU information. The KGB pointed out that the U.S. Central Intelligence Agency (CIA) was already providing some help to the anti-PDPA rebels. The American president Jimmy Carter had authorized the aid in a secret finding in July 1979. That was six months before the first Soviet troops entered.

With all of those successes, it must have seemed logical to the KGB to think that Soviet forces could easily snuff out any U.S. influence in Afghanistan. Afghanistan was a nearby country, bordering the Central Asian Soviet republics of Uzbekistan and Tajikistan. You could drive overland from Moscow to Kabul.

In Afghanistan, the ruling PDPA had two factions, with the radical faction, the Khalq, running the country in 1978 and 1979. Prime Minister Hafizullah Amin overthrew President Muhammad Taraki in September 1979. Both were from the Khalq faction and swore by communist ideals. Both Taraki and Amin had begged the Soviets to come into their country to help put down the resistance to the PDPA.

Thus, the Soviet political leaders were not ready for the political, religious, and military resistance to their invasion of the country. Military intelligence specialists warned about the lack of resources and the small number of troops they were putting in. Even so, Soviet lead-

Both Brezhnev and Carter apparently saw Afghanistan as one more conflict in the cold war. As the situation developed, that is how much of the U.S. public came to see it as well.

The Russian movie *9th Company* (2005) was based on actual events during the Soviets' war in Afghanistan and was Russia's entry for the Academy Award for Best Foreign Language Film that same year. *9th Company* has had financial success in Russia and gained critical acclaim abroad while portraying the heroism of soldiers, conveying the futility of war. *(Gemini Film/Photofest)*

ers felt confident that they could take over Afghanistan the same way that Soviet troops had helped set up a Communist regime in Mongolia years before.

The Soviets did not know how to analyze the situation in Afghanistan. They tried to apply concepts that had little to do with the actual history of Afghanistan. They had not encountered a country with two Communist Parties, each headed by a different tribal leader, each claiming to represent the best pathway to a socialist revolution. The Khalq and Parcham factions were both based on ideology and personal loyalty. And the so-called radical group was headed by a leader the Soviets thought was a U.S. puppet because he had gone to college in the United States.

Other problems in figuring out Afghanistan faced the Soviets. Soviet leaders did not take into account the ethnic and tribal history of the country. They ignored the strong local control, the hatred for

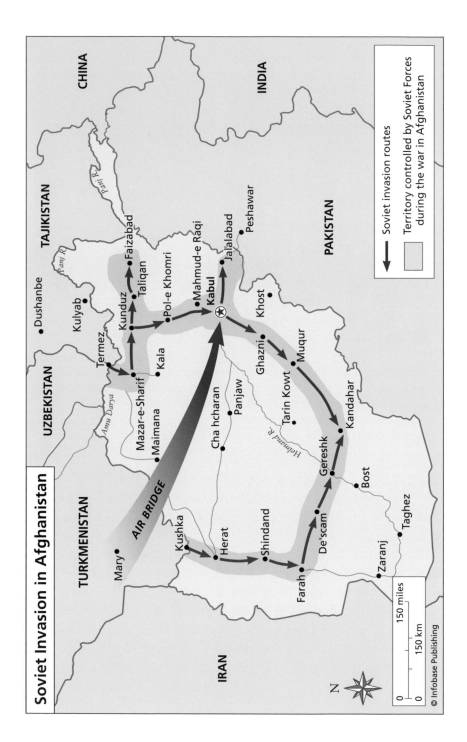

Soviet Invasion in Afghanistan

CHINA

INDIA

TAJIKISTAN

PAKISTAN

• Dushanbe

Kulyab

Faizabad

Peshawar

Taliqan

Jalalabad

Kunduz

Pol-e Khomri

Mahmud-e Rāqi

Panj R.

Kabul

Khost

Termez

UZBEKISTAN

Kala

Ghazni

Muqur

Mazar-e-Sharif

Amu Darya

Maimana

Panjaw

Tarin Kowt

Kandahar

Cha hcharan

Gereshk

Bost

AIR BRIDGE

Helmand R.

TURKMENISTAN

Kushka

Herat

Shindand

De'scam

Taghez

Mary•

Farah

Zaranj

IRAN

N

Soviet invasion routes

Territory controlled by Soviet Forces
during the war in Afghanistan

150 miles

150 km

0

0

© Infobase Publishing

foreigners, and the influence of Islam in the country. Afghans would see Soviet troops as infidels, not as supporters of reforms that would help the poor in the country. Gradually, Soviet military commanders began to understand and report on the importance of the religious factor in their struggle, but by then it was too late.

As mentioned, both Taraki and Amin asked for Soviet aid to maintain order and to help them institute land reform and other socialist measures. Then, in the September 1979 coup, Amin had Taraki killed. The Soviets did not trust Amin and thought he might be a U.S. agent. So with the help of army officers, the Soviets supported a coup that threw out Amin. They replaced him with an exiled leader of the gradualist faction of the PDPA, Babrak Karmal. Karmal welcomed the Soviet troops that arrived on the same day he took over power in the capital.

The Soviet's Fortieth Army spearheaded the invasion in December 1979, right after the coup that put Karmal in power. The 360th Motor Rifle Division led one prong of the invasion to the east. The western force was headed by the 66th Motor Rifle Division with troops from the 357th Motor Rifle Division, heading south toward Herat. Through the night, troops poured into the country. By the time Babrak Karmal issued a formal request for Soviet aid, between 15,000 and 20,000 Soviet troops were already in Afghanistan.

In Afghanistan, the best months to fight were in the spring and fall. In the winter, snow covered the mountain passes and made it difficult for soldiers to retreat from a losing battle; in the summer, the oppressive heat and drought made fighting very difficult. When the Soviets invaded in December 1979, there was very little resistance at first. But in the spring, some tribal leaders organized large armies, called *lashkars,* that attacked Soviet units. The Soviet artillery and aircraft could easily defeat such groups, so tribal leaders decided to support various mujahideen groups.

Some Soviet military analysts estimated they would need 30 or more divisions to take over Afghanistan and bring stability. But they never could supply much more than five divisions because of the broken-down road system. Soviet troops relied on trucks and railway lines for supplies, and they could only get enough food, equipment, and ammunition to support a few divisions at a time.

The Soviets at first simply hoped to be able to prevent foreign invasion from Iran or Pakistan and let the Afghan army fight the insurgents. The Soviets had expected that the Afghan army would fight

POOR SOVIET PREPARATION

Soviet troops had been trained for a possible war against western European armies and the U.S. Army. They did not have any antiguerrilla training. Furthermore, since their theoretical mission was to protect civilians from antigovernment resistance fighters, they soon found themselves in a difficult spot.

Instead of protecting civilians, they had to end up fighting against civilians, sometimes bombing and destroying civilian facilities to prevent guerrilla bands from operating in some regions. Since the rebels would strike and retreat into the mountains, Soviet troops had to repeatedly win the same ground. Heavy equipment like tanks and armored vehicles gave the guerrillas handy targets.

Soviet goals in Afghanistan were not made clear. The Limited Contingent of Soviet Forces in Afghanistan (LCSFA), which is how they referred to their presence in Afghanistan, entered with one set of goals, but those goals were soon changed. Their first mission was to help support the PDPA government. Then the mission changed to help in the overthrow of Amin and to replace him with Babrak Karmal. Soon, the mission changed again.

The LCSFA ended up serving as the armed force to support the Afghan government in its civil war against the mujahideen. The idea that they were protecting a socialist revolution on the ground seemed like a high-minded ideal. But the reality was that they were simply helping to prop up another unpopular central government in Afghanistan.

against the mujahideen and the Soviet army would have the job of protecting the main routes into the country from potential invaders. However, the Afghan army could not handle the mujahideen, and the Soviets had to face that job.

The mujahideen were local groups with local leaders, armed with outmoded weapons. Although loosely organized into seven groups supported from Pakistan and four much weaker groups supported from Iran, the mujahideen was made up of hundreds of small bands, each operating quite independently. Most of the guerrillas fought near their own homes and were led by local leaders such as prominent family members or tribal or village chiefs. Religious leaders like mullahs and imams sometimes came along, but the chiefs of armed bands were usually not the religious leaders.

The Soviet troops were unprepared for mountain fighting, just as U.S. troops had little training or experience for war in the Vietnamese countryside. Experts in both the United States and the Soviet Union saw the Soviet problems in Afghanistan as parallel to the U.S. trouble in Vietnam. Some even called Afghanistan "the Russian Vietnam."

A remnant of the failed Soviet occupation in the 1980s, this abandoned and ruined Russian T-55B MBT tank sits near Bagram Air Base in Afghanistan. *(Department of Defense)*

Because the mujahideen usually fought close to home, they could get food, water, and shelter easily. Relatives would take in the wounded and care for them. At first, the weapons they fought with included Lee-Enfield .303 rifles left over from World War I or even Martini-Henry rifles from the 1880s. When the United States first supplied the mujahideen, they bought up stocks of these old weapons and sent them in through Pakistan. The idea was that the Soviets would not be able to trace the aid to the United States as easily as if the United States sent in modern guns.

After learning some of the facts on the ground, the Soviets began to attack the local support structure that helped out the mujahideen fighters. They used their helicopters and air force to start bombing orchards, farms, villages, and livestock to be able to break up the food

An Afghan mujahideen demonstrates the position used to fire a handheld surface-to-air missile, one of the early Stingers provided by the United States to help drive out the Soviets. *(Department of Defense)*

and shelter supply of the guerrillas. An estimated 5 to 5.5 million Afghans fled into Pakistan and another 2 million became displaced persons, or internal refugees, inside Afghanistan. Almost half of the population of the country fled from their homes.

Of course, these sorts of attacks only angered the population and made them hate the Soviets even more. But the Soviet tactics did disrupt the mujahideen and forced them to carry their own supplies with them and be more mobile and range farther away from their local communities. In the mid-1980s, it seemed possible that the Soviets might win a victory, even a very costly one, and establish some sort of control over the countryside.

Soviet tactics called for staying more than 300 meters away from the enemy. The mujahideen fired rifles and shoulder-launched anti-tank grenades in a line of sight, with the range of such weapons usually limited to about 300 meters. If the Soviet forces had a longer distance to the enemy, it would give them an advantage since they could fire at much longer ranges from their tanks and artillery in a ballistic arc with standoff weapons, rather than in a flat trajectory.

WEAPONS FROM OUTSIDE

Foreign aid to the mujahideen flowing through the Pakistani intelligence agency Inter-Services Intelligence (ISI) led to a busy arms trade in Pakistan. When a mujahideen leader received military aid, it was not always the sort of ammunition that he needed for his weapons. Some of the leaders would sell the guns or ammunition in Pakistan, then use the funds to buy the sort of guns and ammunition they needed. This led to a thriving arms market in the western regions of Pakistan where the refugees and the mujahideen maintained camps and training grounds.

The Americans provided shoulder-launched weapons that fired a heat-seeking missile. These weapons helped bring down the heavy Soviet helicopter gunships. The mujahideen were particularly pleased to receive supplies of Stinger and Blowpipe missiles from the United States after 1986.

Perhaps the most bizarre aspect of the U.S. arming of the mujahideen can be seen in the movie *Charlie Wilson's War*. It tells the story of U.S. Congressman Charlie Wilson, an obscure Democrat from Texas of whom it had been said his greatest achievement was getting reelected. He became so moved by the plight of the Afghan people in their struggle with the Soviets that he began a quiet effort to aid the mujahideen. He first convinced a CIA agent to support him and then managed to send billions of dollars to help arm the mujahideen by hiding the appropriations in bills that his fellow Congressmen paid little or no attention to. (Charlie Wilson died at age 76 on February 10, 2010.)

The Vietnamese had been able to shoot down almost 4,000 U.S. helicopters with much more primitive weapons. The Chinese supplied the mujahideen with the same kind of guns they had sent to Vietnam, including 23-mm antiaircraft guns. However, the mujahideen did not have the same success with these weapons as the Vietnamese had 15 years before and so came to rely on the high-tech American-made weapons. Critics have since pointed out that many of the mujahideen armed with the help of Charlie Wilson and other politicians' incompetence in the 1980s went on to become the Taliban who took over Afghanistan in the 1990s. According to a number of insiders, Charlie Wilson played a significant part in getting the Soviet Union to abandon Afghanistan.

The mujahideen would take cover in orchards, small villages, or rocky country, and the Soviets would try to clear all cover 300 meters on each side of roads, so that their standoff weapons would have an advantage. While the method worked, it meant that much of the crops, homes, villages, and other structures in the countryside had to be destroyed.

For a while, the Soviet tactics had some success. The combination of destruction of local support and the clearing of cover began to work. The Soviets began to control some of the countryside. But the price they paid was to earn even more hatred from the Afghan people and to drive millions into exile in Pakistan.

Both Pakistan and Iran began to aid the mujahideen. When the United States, Britain, Saudi Arabia, Egypt, and other countries provided aid to the mujahideen to oppose the Soviet army, they sent the funding and weapons through Pakistan. Pakistan was ready to help by secretly funneling the support. The reason the Pakistanis helped was because they feared that a strong Soviet-supported state in Afghanistan would hurt their own security.

Pakistan had already fought more than one war against India, and India received regular aid from the Soviets. Pakistani leaders could imagine that they would be trapped between Soviet-supported states on both sides if the Soviets won control of Afghanistan. The ISI collected money and supplies from foreign countries such as the United States. Then the ISI sent the aid to one of the seven mujahideen organizations that operated inside Pakistan.

If guerrilla bands in Afghanistan wanted aid, they had to line up with one or another of the ISI-supported organizations. The Pakistanis made sure that the organizations receiving the most support were those that were Islamic and most strongly anti-Soviet. This meant that most of the aid went to the groups led by Islamic fundamentalists. The support strengthened the religious leaders among the mujahideen.

The covert way that U.S. aid reached the mujahideen led to an entirely unintended result. First of all, since U.S. authorities wanted to be able to deny to the public in the United States and around the world that they were sending aid, it was all sent through the ISI in Pakistan. While some of the Afghan mujahideen may have realized that the original source of the aid was the United States, the Pakistanis and the religious factions could take credit for the aid.

Furthermore, most of the aid went to the most radical Islamic groups, including groups that were extremely opposed to U.S. influence in the Middle East. Behind the scenes, a relief organization established with Saudi money provided pensions and medical help

These abandoned Soviet military artillery pieces, most of them unserviceable, were found as the NATO forces moved into Afghanistan during Operation Enduring Freedom. *(Department of Defense)*

to families of religious fighters. Headed by Osama bin Laden, this organization gained influence and friends within the more radical Islamic groups.

Most of the mujahideen did not really fight as highly organized guerrilla units with a chain of command and large-scale planning. Instead, their tactics consisted of hit-and-run ambushes and quick retreats by little bands of a few dozen or few hundred headed by one man. Two of the more successful units that operated like guerrilla armies were those in the north of the country headed by Ahmad Shah Massoud and by Ismail Khan, both minority Tajiks. Massoud headed an army of perhaps 3,000 fighters. His group was able to attack Soviet air bases and major fortresses. Khan's front was run by ex-army officers. Both groups had full-time, paid soldiers, with ranks of officers, rather than single chieftains running independent bands.

Some estimates put the number of Afghan fighters against the Soviets as high as 200,000 part-time mujahideen. A number of factors prevented this huge number of guerrilla fighters from immediately destroying the Soviet troops. Much of the mujahideen's time and a great deal of their arms and ammunition were used in intergroup feuds. Some of the fighters were clearly in merely for money or loot. This allowed the government to actually buy out numbers of leaders and whole bands of mujahideen.

Furthermore, after a few defections of army officers early on, no major army units defected to the resistance after the mid-1980s. Most of the guerrillas had little or no formal training in guerrilla warfare, most were commanded by local chieftains rather than knowledgeable officers, and most were incapable of mounting large-scale attacks. For all of these reasons, the Soviets continued to hope that they might succeed.

Americans in the 1980s tended to see support for the mujahideen as a good thing, because the fighters were wearing down the Soviets and resisting a foreign invasion. But behind the scenes, the reality of the mujahideen was something else.

While Americans, Saudis, and Chinese all supported one or more branches of the mujahideen through Pakistan as an effort to oppose Soviet expansion, few of the outsiders understood exactly who the mujahideen were. In fact, many of the mujahideen obtained funds through the export of opium, the base for heroin. Many of the mujahideen were perfectly willing to use terror tactics, such as planting bombs in city streets, schools, and mosques. They were so divided among themselves and aligned with obscure political and religious factions based in Pakistan and so many of them were committed to radical Islam that it was not clear to outsiders exactly who they were supporting.

The Soviet war in Afghanistan had severe repercussions in the Soviet Union. With both the Afghans and the Soviet soldiers thinking of the Soviet army as invaders rather than liberators, the war became very unpopular in the Soviet Union. Civilians did not welcome home the Soviet veterans who returned. Prominent outspoken critics of the Soviet regime highlighted rumors of Soviet atrocities in Afghanistan. Inside the Soviet Union, in the Central Asian republics like Tajikistan and Uzbekistan, the fact that the Soviet army was fighting against neighboring Muslims helped fuel a rise in Islamic fundamentalism. The Soviets were horrified to see that movement grow inside the Soviet Union itself. The Soviet fight in Afghanistan strengthened the movement for independence in the region of Chechnya that lay within the borders of the Russian Federation itself.

Afghan air force jets fly in review in 2007 during a parade commemorating the 15th anniversary of the mujahideen's retaking of Kabul from the Soviet-installed communist government. *(Department of Defense)*

Each side tried to cut off the supplies of the other side. Thus, it became a war over logistics and had become a stalemate. Inside the Soviet Union, between 1981 and 1985, three older Soviet leaders could not decide on a new policy. In 1985, Mikhail Gorbachev, a much younger and more reform-minded leader, came to power in the Soviet Union. By 1986, Gorbachev decided that the Soviet army should withdraw from Afghanistan and not take on any major battles in order to minimize casualties and to limit the damage. Later evidence suggests that in 1985 the mujahideen may have been close to being destroyed, but Gorbachev's decision to turn the war over to the Afghan government was final.

The Soviets got out, and the Afghan regime was able to last a few more years, outlasting the Soviet Union itself. The last Soviet combat troops withdrew from Afghanistan by February 15, 1989. The mujahideen were so divided into different competing organizations that they had difficulty mounting a strong attack on the PDPA government that the Soviets left behind. The regime of Najibullah, supported by the Soviets, would last for three more years after the Soviets departed.

With the withdrawal of Soviet forces, the United States no longer took a direct interest in Afghanistan's internal affairs. Americans liked to believe that the Soviet problem in Afghanistan helped cause the collapse of the Soviet government. The Soviet Union broke up into separate countries in 1990. With the cold war over, U.S. foreign policy no longer had to focus on the expansion of Soviet power. However, it would eventually become clear that U.S. help to the mujahideen had disastrous long-term results that hurt U.S. interests.

THE ORIGINS
OF AL-QAEDA

When Americans learned of al-Qaeda in 2001, it seemed to be a strange and dedicated group of fanatics who did not understand American life at all. Americans sought answers to numerous questions.

How did al-Qaeda come to hate America? Why did they settle on a refuge in Afghanistan? How were they linked to the cruel Taliban regime that governed Afghanistan in the period from 1996 to 2001? Why did some Muslims join al-Qaeda, while others thought the group was fanatical and led by psychologically disturbed individuals who distorted the teachings of Islam?

At first, most of these questions seemed almost impossible to answer because the organization had operated secretly for years. However, as journalists and intelligence agencies collected information, the story of the organization and how it ended up in Afghanistan began to come out.

The ideas that formed the ideology of al-Qaeda had their origins in an Egyptian movement known as the Muslim Brotherhood. Formally founded in 1928, the group plotted to remove British and other Western influences in Egypt by overthrowing the government. The Muslim Brotherhood attracted young intellectuals in Egypt who felt dissatisfied with their government.

Many believed that Egypt had failed to support the Arabs in Palestine against the Jewish settlers who established Israel. In their resentment of the suppression of dissent in Egypt, some members of the Muslim Brotherhood accepted the idea of overthrowing the Egyptian government. They did not plan a widespread revolution. Instead they hoped to win success by converting Egyptian army officers to their cause. They hoped that the officers would stage a coup.

THE MUSLIM BROTHERHOOD

The Muslim Brotherhood (Society of the Muslim Brothers) was an Islamic revivalist movement established in 1928 in Egypt by Hasan al-Banna, a young schoolteacher. Al-Banna argued that Islam was not simply a system of religion but a whole way of life. He supplemented traditional Islamic education for young boys with military training for a jihad, or holy war. During the 1930s and 1940s, the movement grew in Egypt and became a political party. The party criticized the Egyptian government for not taking a stronger stand against the creation of Israel.

On December 28, 1948, a Brotherhood member, Abdel Meguid Ahmed Hassan, assassinated Egypt's prime minister Mahmud Fahmi Nokrashi. Al-Banna himself was killed by government agents in Cairo in February 1949. The Brotherhood began to demand that Egypt institute sharia, or Islamic law.

In 1954, several members of the Brotherhood attempted to assassinate Egyptian president Gamal Abdel Nasser. The government caught and executed the assassins. In a wholesale roundup, the government also arrested about 4,000 members of the organization.

Nasser granted amnesty to the imprisoned members, but assassination attempts against Nasser continued. In 1966, the Egyptian government arrested more leaders of the Brotherhood and executed some of them for involvement in the plots. The Brotherhood grew more angry when Nasser's successor, Anwar Sadat, signed an agreement with Israel in 1979.

A small group of Brotherhood members, including one recruited by Dr. Zawahiri, assassinated President Sadat in 1981. The government arrested Zawahiri and imprisoned him with other members of the Brotherhood.

Even though the party has been banned in Egypt, they continue to nominate candidates and have taken some seats in the Egyptian parliament under the guise of being independent candidates. The ideas of the Muslim Brotherhood, including hostility toward Israel and Western governments and insistence on enforcing sharia, have influenced other radical Islamic groups around the world.

Ayman al-Zawahiri is a medical doctor from an upper-class Egyptian family. Even as a teenager, he was swept up in the ideas of the Muslim Brotherhood. Among the people that Zawahiri recruited into the Muslim Brotherhood was a young Egyptian army officer. That officer took part in the group that assassinated Anwar Sadat in 1981.

When the Egyptian government arrested the conspirators, the police picked up Zawahiri and held him in jail. As one of the most educated of the prisoners, Zawahiri emerged as a spokesman for the group. In prison, Zawahiri and his fellow prisoners practiced and sharpened their lines of argument and thinking against the influences they saw as preventing Egypt from leading the Muslim world.

After release from prison, Zawahiri shifted his focus from overthrowing the Egyptian government to a more radical view of a worldwide Muslim movement against modernity and the West. Zawahiri formed a group he called Islamic Jihad. He later merged his group with the organization created by Osama bin Laden. In the history of these organizations, Islamic Jihad can be viewed as a radical spin-off of the Muslim Brotherhood.

Osama bin Laden came from a large and wealthy family that was established by his father, a poor laborer who emigrated from Yemen to Saudi Arabia in about 1930. There, he moved up through the construction business until he had his own firm during an era when the Saudis were reaping large profits from the country's many oil wells. Bin Laden's father prospered by building roads, office buildings, government projects, mosques, and other projects, and eventually became the favored contractor and trusted ally of the royal family. Osama bin Laden is believed to have been the 17th of at least 54 of his father's children with 22 wives.

Growing up in Saudi Arabia in a wealthy family in the construction business, Osama bin Laden decided to take his wealth and know-how to help the mujahideen in Afghanistan. During the mujahideen resistance to the Soviets, Osama bin Laden wanted to provide a channel for money to help the Afghans throw out the Soviets. At first, he established what he called the Services Bureau in Peshawar, Pakistan.

Using money from his family and friends, bin Laden's Services Bureau provided money to volunteers who came to fight against the Soviets. The Arab volunteers were usually untrained. Some were misfits, some were thrill-seekers, and some were dedicated to Islam. Most were barely out of high school. Some were funded by their parents, others went on their own.

The Services Bureau gave the fighters a salary, some training, and money for their families (and widows and orphans). Osama bin Laden's regular payments to these young men helped them and their families. At the same time, his money made them dependent on him.

President George H. W. Bush meets with King Fahd at the Royal Pavilion in Saudi Arabia in November 1991 to discuss the probable campaign to remove Iraqi forces from Kuwait. *(George Bush Presidential Library and Museum)*

The Arab volunteers who gathered in Pakistan were sent over to fight in different mujahideen bands. Most of them were not very effective because they tended to be untrained. Often mujahideen commanders would leave the Arab fighters behind after a hit-and-run raid. The Arab fighters often became the rearguard that would be slaughtered by the Soviets. Out of more than an estimated 200,000 mujahideen, there were probably about 3,000 Arab volunteers.

Zawahiri and bin Laden met in Peshawar. Bin Laden had money, organizational ability, and a sense of self-importance that brought him followers. Zawahiri had a strong intellectual foundation and ideas and a hatred for Israel, the United States, and western Europe. Each man developed his own organization, which they formally merged in 1998. Zawahiri's Islamic Jihad had many followers from Egypt. Bin Laden's al-Qaeda organization grew among Arabs from Saudi Arabia and recruits from other countries.

Bin Laden did set up one unit of Arab troops, perhaps 60 or so strong, to fight in Afghanistan. The Pashtun refugees in Peshawar called his little group the Brigade of Strangers. Bin Laden's followers set up a small base over the border in Afghanistan.

The Arab expression meaning "the base" is al-Qaeda. It also means "base" in the sense of an underpinning or foundation or framework. During this period in the mid-1980s, the name became attached to bin Laden's operation.

The base near Jali, a small town in the northeast of Afghanistan, saw little action against the Soviets. The base was at first just a sort of camp in the mountains. Later, bin Laden used his construction background to build cave networks to serve as ammunition depots, barracks, and even a hospital in the mountains of Tora Bora.

Since the Brigade of Strangers was untrained and did not have a military commander, it was very amateurish. However, there was one engagement during which some of bin Laden's unit were able to stand

Pictured is the Khobar Towers, an apartment building where U.S. troops were housed in Khobar, Saudi Arabia, after a terrorist bomb exploded on June 25, 1996, and killed 19 U.S. servicemen. *(Department of Defense)*

off an attack by Soviet troops. Later, bin Laden and his propagandists made a lot of this gunfight, even though bin Laden himself tended to fall sick every time military action threatened. Sometimes Zawahiri would provide him with medicine to help him recover during a firefight.

For a while, bin Laden continued to receive income from his share of the family corporations. During the period of the resistance to the Soviet troops in Afghanistan, bin Laden had the approval of the government of Saudi Arabia. Neither the United States nor Saudi Arabia saw bin Laden as hostile to their interests in this period.

With the withdrawal of the Soviets in 1989, bin Laden returned to Saudi Arabia and the family businesses there. When Saddam Hussein invaded Kuwait on August 2, 1990, the invasion of a neighboring country horrified the Saudi government. The Saudis had a very small army and could not stop Hussein if he decided to move on from Kuwait into their own territory.

The Saudi government called for U.S. aid, and U.S. troops (including females) deployed to Saudi Arabia to prepare for the recapture of Kuwait. The brief Gulf War in 1991 that expelled Hussein's army from Kuwait is covered in another book in this series.

The reaction of bin Laden to the invasion of Kuwait by Iraq was to demand to raise his own army to defend Saudi Arabia against Hussein. He regarded it as a sacrilege to allow Americans into Arabia, the holy land of Islam. The Saudi government was appalled at bin Laden and ordered him to stop arguing.

The Saudis understood that only a large, professional army, not a ragged band of enthusiastic youths with no training, could stop Hussein. If Hussein continued his advance into Saudi Arabia, he would be able to seize the nation's oil fields and control the wealth and power of a much larger empire.

Bin Laden was disgusted with the orders from the Saudi government telling him to be quiet. In order to have a freer field of action, he moved to Sudan, which at that time was governed by an anti-Western Islamic dictatorship.

In the early 1990s, bin Laden set up his own construction businesses in Sudan. The Islamic government of Sudan welcomed bin Laden and his more radical ideas because he brought in large amounts of money. Since he continued to protest the U.S. help to Saudi Arabia, the Saudi government canceled his passport. The Sudanese, however,

THE PERSIAN GULF WAR

Saddam Hussein's Iraqi army quickly overran the small country of Kuwait in August 1990. Over the next six months, American troops and troops from 33 other countries assembled in bases in northern Saudi Arabia, near the border with Kuwait.

The king of Saudi Arabia had invited them, fearing that the Iraqi army would invade Saudi Arabia and seize the rich oil fields in the region near Kuwait. The UN Security Council passed resolutions authorizing the use of force if Hussein did not withdraw from Kuwait.

In the United States, President George Herbert Walker Bush obtained the approval of Congress to use force to remove Hussein's army from Kuwait if he did not pull out voluntarily. On January 16, 1991, Operation Desert Storm began with an intense bombing campaign targeting Iraqi military forces. Within 30 days, American and Coalition air attacks had destroyed 1,300 Iraqi tanks, 1,100 pieces of artillery, and 850 armored personnel carriers.

In a well-planned assault, the Coalition, headed by American general Norman Schwarzkopf, swept into Kuwait and southern Iraq beginning on February 24. The rapid advance of tanks and other armored forces raced forward in a wide arc through the desert. In the first few days of the advance, more than 30,000 Iraqi troops surrendered.

After Kuwait City was liberated from the Iraqis, remnants of the Iraqi army streamed northward. General Schwarzkopf accepted surrender in the field from the Iraqi generals almost exactly 100 hours after the ground attack began. The land battles of the Persian Gulf War had taken four days. The Coalition troops did not pursue the Iraqi army as it retreated deeper into Iraq, because the UN and the Coalition governments had agreed only to free Kuwait from the invasion, not to conquer all of Iraq.

Although Kuwait had been liberated and Saudi Arabia had been protected, Osama bin Laden criticized the ruling family of Saudi Arabia for allowing American and European troops into the kingdom.

were glad to have him in their country at first. Using his money and construction experience, he built factories and highways. While he was based in Sudan, bin Laden began to develop ideas for concerted attacks on Americans, several of which were later carried out, including two attacks on American embassies in Africa.

Even though bin Laden was able to plan his operations from his offices in Sudan and was welcomed by the Sudanese government, he became dissatisfied with the Sudan regime. He criticized the Sudanese because they continued to tolerate such Western practices as movie theaters. They also practiced tolerance for various sects of Islam. He was also angry because the regime refused to endorse a jihad against the United States. Among his other problems, bin Laden managed his business ventures in Sudan very poorly. The businesses continued to drain his fortune rather than show a profit.

As bin Laden's anti-American plans emerged, the United States and Egypt put pressure on the Sudanese government to either arrest bin Laden or to expel him. Finally, in 1996, the Sudanese decided to confiscate his properties and force him to leave the country. He claimed he lost investments worth $160 million in Sudan, but other estimates put the amount between $20 and $30 million.

His family cut him off from further funds from Saudi Arabia, so he no longer had the vast fortune available. In fact, when he left the country, he was probably reduced to poverty, although outsiders thought he was immensely wealthy. He still had lots of wealthy friends in Saudi Arabia.

When the Sudanese told him to leave, he decided to flee to Afghanistan. The Sudanese government paid to hire a plane to take bin Laden and some of his family and close supporters to Afghanistan on May 18, 1996. A group of former mujahideen near Jalalabad invited him to stay there. After the Taliban took power later the same year, he moved to Kandahar, under the protection of the central Taliban leadership.

Believing that bin Laden still had access to a vast fortune, the Taliban leaders of Afghanistan allowed him to support a training camp. They provided him with Tarnak Farms, a disused compound for his family and aides, but they did not approve of his plans to attack American facilities. Furthermore, they tried to prevent him from giving interviews to journalists or drawing attention to his virulent anti-American views. Despite the fact that he was a stateless refugee who almost all countries would refuse to allow to enter, he ignored the Taliban's restrictions.

On February 23, 1998, bin Laden publicized an edict or fatwa against the United States, after working out the language with Ayman al-Zawahiri as part of their plan to merge al-Qaeda and Islamic Jihad. Meanwhile, planning groups that he had set up while in Sudan went ahead

U.S. Air Force Honor Guard pallbearers carry the flag-draped coffin containing the remains of a U.S.A.F. sergeant killed in the terrorist bombing attack on the U.S. embassy in Nairobi, Kenya, on August 7, 1998. *(Department of Defense)*

with bombing the American embassies in Kenya and Tanzania. Bin Laden continued to publicize his message of attack on the United States.

In retaliation for the explosions at the embassies, President Bill Clinton of the United States ordered two retaliatory strikes by missiles. Due to faulty intelligence, the strikes had virtually no impact on bin Laden or al-Qaeda. A factory in Sudan that manufactured medicine was hit because U.S. intelligence officials incorrectly thought that bin Laden had built it to make poison gas.

U.S. missiles also hit bin Laden's terrorist training camp near Khost in Afghanistan. The missiles destroyed some tents and killed six trainees but none of the al-Qaeda leadership. Some of the missiles failed to detonate. Bin Laden's group was later able to sell the unexploded missiles for a profit.

Although the leaders of the Taliban had resented bin Laden imposing on their hospitality by using their country to plan attacks on the United States, when the United States retaliated by striking a base on their territory, they began to change their minds. They had planned to turn bin Laden over to the Saudis to be taken home for trial. But

ATTACKS ON U.S. EMBASSIES IN KENYA AND TANZANIA

On August 7, 1998, two near-simultaneous bombing attacks on U.S. embassies represented the beginning of al-Qaeda's overt actions against the United States. The two bombs went off in Nairobi, Kenya, and Dar es Salaam, Tanzania. The U.S. embassy in Nairobi was right in the center of the busy downtown area. The bomb there killed 291 people, including 12 Americans, and wounded about 5,000. The bomb in the capital of Tanzania killed 10 and wounded 77.

Planning for the attacks had begun as early as December 1993, before Osama bin Laden's move from Sudan to Afghanistan. In January 1994, bin Laden got the reports of the first planning. He worked with a military committee that decided that the embassy in Nairobi would be an ideal target. A car bomb could be parked right on the crowded street in front of the embassy. Several investigations and other problems delayed the plan.

In early August, bin Laden moved out of the city of Kandahar for his hideout in the country, fearing there would be retaliations for the two bombings. He prepared declarations taking credit for the two bombings and had them sent just before the bombs went off. Two trucks loaded with bombs drove up to the embassies at almost the same time on the morning of August 7, 1998. The messages taking credit were sent by fax to London.

The Quran specifically forbids the killing of innocents. Around the world, Muslims condemned the two bombings as pointless slaughter.

after the missile strike, they hardened their attitude toward the United States. The Taliban continued to shelter bin Laden.

The war in Afghanistan cannot be understood without an understanding of the rise of the Taliban, the regime that provided shelter to bin Laden and Zawahiri.

THE RISE OF
THE TALIBAN

In 1994, while Burhanuddin Rabbani still ruled in Kabul, dozens of petty chieftains and their bands roamed freely in the Pashtun southern and eastern provinces. The road from Kandahar to Pakistan, an old caravan route and now a truck route, fell into local chiefs' hands. They set up barricades on the road and would charge truck drivers a toll or bribe to pass through. The truck drivers of Kandahar were outraged as the lawless conditions ruined their business.

While not exactly anarchy, it was clear that the country had broken up into groups of provinces controlled by local leaders and warlords, with some provinces under the gangster rule of bands of roving gunmen.

The mujahideen leader Gulbuddin Hekmatyar controlled a small region to the south and east of Kabul. Another army, under Ismail Khan, had its base in Herat. In the north, the Uzbek warlord Rashid Dostum held six provinces. A sporadic civil war continued, especially as Hekmatyar made several attempts to throw out the Rabbani regime in Kabul.

The southeastern region around Kandahar had dozens of bandits and petty ex-mujahideen warlords who competed for control over small patches of territory. In 1994, Hekmatyar and Khan attacked Kabul, but Massoud held out for a while and kept the capital in the hands of the Tajik-dominated regime of Rabbani.

Pashtuns in the south and east were outraged at Tajik control of the capital. Most people in the region were tired of years of warfare and disruption. Local leaders in the Pashtun southeast hoped for some solution. They were supported especially by the truck drivers of Kandahar who demanded that the bandits who blocked the highways be stopped.

The seven parties organized in Afghanistan represented competing ethnic groups and reflected traditional lines of loyalty to specific families. They also varied in their religious and political views. While these parties organized the mujahideen, Afghan boys who were too young to be sent to the front lived in the refugee camps in Pakistan. Many went to the madrassas, schools organized by radical Islamic Pakistani Pashtun teachers.

The generation of teenage boys and young men who fled as orphans or with one or more parents to Pakistan in the period from 1979 to 1989 would return in vast numbers in the mid- and late 1990s. They would seize power in 1996 in most of the provinces of Afghanistan and establish a new regime. This generation of students—*talibs* in Pashtun—would form the militias of the Taliban in the 1990s. Their rule became known as that of the Taliban.

The head of a local madrassa near Kandahar, Mullah Mohammed Omar, emerged in this period as a leader. He was a reclusive and secretive religious figure who refused to have his picture taken or to talk to visiting journalists. Omar remained a difficult person to understand from the outside.

Legends and rumors surrounded Omar's influence in the chaotic period of the early 1990s. One story attributes his early fame to an incident in which he led a few armed students in the rescue of two local girls being raped. The same group was reputed to later rescue a boy about to be raped by local army officers. In the region near Kandahar, people turned to Omar for help with local problems. At the same time, by September 1994, the government of Pakistan hoped to open the road to Turkestan via the southern route for overland trade.

The Pakistani government, planning to pacify the road to Kandahar, helped Omar's student followers seize ammunition at the Spin Baldak truck stop near the Pakistani border. Then, the Pakistanis pushed a truck convoy in. It was held up on October 29 to November 4, 1994, by three commanders from the Kabul army of Rabbani. They demanded bribes. Omar's student militias (Taliban), with weapons from Spin Baldak, freed the trucks. Then the Taliban moved in and took over the whole city of Kandahar. They captured the airport and more weapons.

Kandahar is the second-largest city in Afghanistan. The Taliban cleared the chains that had blocked the highway and reduced the tolls

MADRASSAS AND *TALIBS*

Among the 1.5 to 2.2 million Pashtun refugees inside Pakistan, madrassas were set up. *Madrassa* is Arabic for "a place where learning takes place" and simply refers to a school; even girls attend madrassas, although they are schooled apart from boys. In madrassas throughout the Muslim world, the course of study may have a strong religious element, but many other subjects are also taught. However, the madrassas in Pakistan attended by the boys from Afghanistan tended to be dominated by extremely conservative religious Muslims. Most of the teachers could not even read or write. The schools were all male, and the teachings represented a radical version of Islam, with an extremely anti-Western and antimodern viewpoint. Beyond that, they taught the young boys that they would be carrying out the Islamic concept of jihad if they sacrificed their lives in killing infidels.

A generation of boys over the period from 1983 to 1995 went through these schools as students or *talibs*. A boy born in Afghanistan from 1975 to 1985 could spend all of his childhood and school years in refugee camps and madrassas in Pakistan.

Young Afghan boys study the Quran at a madrassa. *(Photo by Lizette Potgieter/Shutterstock)*

to two. By December 1994, convoys started coming through. The Taliban regime was under way.

Afghan students, some 12,000 to 20,000, flooded in from Pakistan to join the Taliban. The Taliban begin implementing their version of sharia, Islamic law. They prohibited all arts and music, required women to be veiled from head to toe, and stopped the playing of all sports. Within a few months, they had control of 12 of the country's 31 provinces.

Since many of these *talibs* had been trained in Pakistani madrassas, they combined their own culture with the ideas of the madrassa teachers, most of whom belonged to the Deobandi branch of Islam. Deobandi is a branch of Islam that seeks to purify Islam by discarding un-Islamic things and concentrating on the Quran, at the same time discarding Western influences.

DEOBANDI

Most of the teachers in the madrassas in Pakistan were members of the Deobandi sect of Islam. The sect is named for the town of Deoband, about 100 miles north of Delhi, India, where the sect's first school was set up in 1867. The school reflected the tradition of Muslims in India who were opposed to British rule and who believed in a very austere version of Islam.

Members of the Deobandi madrassas hoped to purify Islam by getting rid of un-Islamic additions to the faith and reverting to the practices of the prophet Muhammad. They reject any practices that they see as derived from Western influences. Although the Deobandi sect had its beginnings in the Sunni branch of Islam, its views depart from those of most of the rest of the Sunni.

The Deobandi view holds that a proper Muslim should be loyal first to his religion and only secondarily to the country of his citizenship. Furthermore, Deobandi views hold that Muslims should not pay any attention to national boundaries. Also, they have an obligation and a right to wage jihad to protect Muslims in any country in the world.

The Deobandi hold a very restrictive view of women and regard the Shia minority (the dominant religion in Iran, but a minority in Pakistan and Afghanistan) as non-Muslims or heretics. The fundamentalist Deobandi group provided the theoretical basis for the ideas of the Taliban. Most Taliban leaders and many of the troops had attended Deobandi-dominated madrassas in Pakistan.

Afghanistan Civil War, 1990s

Northern Alliance
- Dostum's territory
- Massoud's territory

Concentration of Afghan refugees

Border of Afghanistan

Kandahar Home base of Taliban movement

Suspected terrorist training camps bombed by the United States in 1998

© Infobase Publishing

In 1995, civil war between different mujahideen factions, with multiple betrayals and breakdowns of alliances, allowed the Taliban to establish control in the Pashtun provinces. Massoud continued to hold a section of Kabul for a period, but the rising forces of the Taliban soon drove him out. In 1996, at a meeting of religious leaders known as an ulema, Mullah Omar was named emir of Afghanistan. The Taliban claimed that Afghanistan was now an emirate.

This claim shocked many traditional Muslims who did not recognize the ulema that had elevated Omar. They said it was not a legitimate body. Rabbani received aid from Russia, India, and the Central Asian republics. Iran sought to support some of the Afghan militias who shared Iran's Shia faith. At the same time, the Taliban continued to get aid from Pakistan and Saudi Arabia. International observers became worried that Afghanistan could turn into a major war zone between the forces of Iran and Russia and India on one hand and Pakistan and Saudi Arabia on the other.

On September 26, 1996, the Taliban swept into Kabul, while Massoud escaped north with armor and artillery. At first, many Afghans in Kabul believed the Taliban regime would bring peace to the country. They hoped the new leaders would end the years of bloodshed and rule by petty warlords. Outside governments, such as that of the United States, adopted a wait-and-see attitude, also hoping that the Taliban would stabilize the country. They would soon be disappointed.

Taliban militia immediately took Najibullah, the deposed Marxist leader, from the UN compound. They beat, castrated, and shot him. They hung his bloodied body for everyone to see from a concrete traffic post near the UN building and the palace in downtown Kabul.

Although Kabul was in chaos, it was still a cosmopolitan city with foreign residents, consuls, and journalists. The atrocity killing of the former president Najibullah was reported around the world. Westerners and Muslims alike denounced the Taliban for seizing Najibullah and letting a mob kill him without trial.

The Taliban immediately began to impose their version of sharia in Kabul. One of the first changes that caught the attention of the world was the violation of women's rights. The regime immediately expelled 70,000 women and girl students from schools. Thousands more lost their jobs. To strengthen their forces, the Taliban began bringing in whole busloads of students from the madrassas of Pakistan where Afghan refugees still lived.

The same ulema that had decided to make Afghanistan an emirate also named Mullah Omar as the emir, head of state and commander of the faithful in 1997. By 1997, the Taliban controlled 22 provinces. Omar was head of an inner council, or *shura*, based in Kandahar.

Meanwhile, in the north, a rival Tajik regime known as the Islamic State of Afghanistan was able to retain control of about 10 percent of the country. Burhanuddin Rabbani, who had been the president of all of Afghanistan from 1992 to 1996, stayed on as the political head of this government. He was still supported by the organized mujahideen army under Ahmad Shah Massoud.

Both Omar's Taliban regime and the Rabbani government tried to fill Afghanistan's seat at the United Nations, but it remained empty. Much of the country had no effective government at all. In 1999, the Taliban announced that it would draft a constitution, but none was produced. The civil war between the Tajik government of Rabbani and

TALIBAN VALUES

When the Taliban emerged, their values were drawn from a mix of radical Islamic ideas, derived from the madrassas of Pakistan, and Pashtunwali, a nonwritten law, or honor code, of the rural Pashtun people. Pashtunwali is a moral code that outlines how people should live in social groups and how they should behave personally and to each other. The code has ideas regarding honor, solidarity, shame, hospitality, and personal and group revenge. The defense of honor is an obligation, even if it requires sacrifice of one's own life. Some of the ideas of Pashtunwali run counter to traditional Islamic values of sharia, the code of behavior derived from the Quran and from Islamic teaching.

The Quran prohibits the killing of innocent civilians, but under Pashtunwali, the family of an enemy may be slaughtered. When the central government of Afghanistan imposed land reform and disrupted traditional dominance of specific families and tribes, many Pashtun people saw these changes as violations of Pashtunwali.

Among other violations of traditional Islamic law and custom, the Taliban would burn schools where girls had been educated, believing that education of women violated sharia. Burning of schools is a violation of the Quran.

The Taliban believed in *takfir,* that is the excommunication of Muslims who disagreed with them, allowing them to be killed. This doctrine was used to justify the slaughters in Shia regions of the country. Bin Laden also believed in this heretical doctrine. Al-Qaeda and Osama bin Laden accepted the concept of suicide missions, and the Taliban came to accept this doctrine as well. Suicide is forbidden by the Quran.

the Taliban kept up over the next several years. During the war, the Taliban regime strengthened its hold on parts of the country.

The Taliban controlled the flow of information, so it was very difficult for the outside world to find out exactly what was going on inside the country. However, stories leaked out, and some journalists and observers were able to verify some rumors of the horrors going on. Reports that the Taliban had eased its rule in some areas of the country in the year 2000 were soon proven wrong by word of worse abuses.

Members of the Taliban regime simply executed without trial those who it suspected of opposing its regime, sometimes with targeted killings and sometimes after arresting and torturing the opponents. In January 2001, the Taliban summarily executed an estimated 300 men and teenage boys of the Hazara (Shia) minority in Bamiyan's Yakawlang district.

There were reports of other, larger-scale atrocities, ethnic cleansing, shooting of civilians, and slaughters of captured troops. In the town of Mazar-e Sharif, on August 7, 1998, the Taliban militia went house to house, pulling all men and boys into the streets and shooting them on the spot. They left the bodies in the street and shot any family members who tried to come out to pick up the bodies for burial. They would enter homes and kill everyone, including children and babies. Altogether, an estimated 5,000 to 6,000 civilians were killed in this single atrocity. From the point of view of the Taliban, the residents of Mazar-e Sharif were not true Muslims, as they were mostly Shia.

When the Taliban religious police and courts enforced the ultra-conservative interpretation of sharia, they would carry out punishments such as stoning to death, flogging, or amputation of hands for theft. Public executions went on in the national sports stadium in Kabul. For minor infractions, such as that of a woman walking in public without being accompanied by a male relative, Taliban special police simply judged the offense right on the spot. They would then carry out the punishment, such as a beating with a cane.

The Taliban military tactics forced civilians to evacuate their homes, as they would bombard civilian areas. They would harass, arrest, and sometimes kill members of international relief organizations. Any recruiting to a non-Muslim religion was forbidden. If any Muslim converted to Christianity or Judaism, the crime was punishable by death.

CHRONOLOGY, 1989–2001

1989
- Soviets complete their withdrawal from Afghanistan. Najibullah, head of PDPA, in control since 1986, continues in power.

1989
- Mujahideen parties in Pakistan select Mojadeddi to act as president of an Afghan interim government.

1992
- Najibullah regime collapses and yields to mujahideen.

1992
- Mojadeddi rules in Kabul for two months, then is deposed in favor of Burhanuddin Rabbani.

1992–96
- Mujahideen regime under Rabbani is supported by Massoud. This group faces a civil war with Hekmatyar, whose more radical group fought against the Soviets from Pakistan.

1996
- Taliban assume power in Kabul in September 1996; hang Najibullah who had taken refuge in UN compound; govern from Kandahar.

1996
- Taliban council of clerics runs most of Afghanistan, headed by Mohammed Omar. Taliban institutes severe and distorted version of sharia.

1996
- In August, bin Laden moves from Sudan to Afghanistan and declares a fatwa against the United States.

1997
- Mullah Mohammed Omar is named head of state and commander of the faithful.

1997–2001
- Taliban regime alienates all outside support except for Saudi Arabia, United Arab Emirates, and Pakistan; suppresses basic human rights; commits atrocities.

2001
- In September, two days before 9/11, a group organized by al-Qaeda assassinates Massoud in Takhar Province.

All of these practices flew in the face of traditional Muslim values. They represented a radical Islamic set of ideas rejected by the majority of Muslims around the world.

Television was banned, as were movies and the playing of any music other than religious chants. Taliban militia went house to house, destroying televisions and satellite receivers. But even though movies and television were banned, many people kept their televisions and video cassette players and watched them in secret. In 2001, the movie *Titanic* became a great hit. People watched the film in their homes. A huge mar-

An Afghan National Army soldier stands guard at the ruins of the two statues of Buddha in the Bamiyan Valley of Afghanistan. During their rule, the Taliban destroyed these statues despite an international effort to save them. *(Department of Defense)*

ket in a slum was nicknamed "Titanic." Some barbers cut hair to match the style worn by Leonardo DiCaprio in that film. *Titanic* T-shirts and other memorabilia were seen everywhere in Kabul. The romantic love story against the background of the tragedy of the shipwreck may have seemed like a way of telling the story of Afghanistan itself.

Although the Taliban regime lasted only about five years, the severe restrictions on human rights were so appalling that almost all governments in the world refused to recognize the regime. Yet the world could only deplore the Taliban's actions. In particular, the world looked on with shock when the Taliban completely destroyed the two monumental sixth-century statues of Buddha at Bamiyan, a UNESCO World Heritage Site. They also destroyed images and many other objects in the National Museum.

Aside from the Taliban regime's harsh and restrictive rules, it differed from other governments in another respect. The Taliban believed in the extreme Islamic view that government itself was unnecessary in a society in which everyone acted in a virtuous way. That is, they believed politics and the usual business of the state in terms of administration were not needed if the population obeyed sharia.

Because the Taliban believed that their most important job was to maintain control and to enforce a moral code, the Taliban regime did not provide any of the usual services common in modern countries, such as health care, utilities, or other public services. Because of this, the importance of foreign-based charities and other nongovernmental organizations (NGOs) became even greater in Afghanistan than in other very poor countries of the world.

The Afghan people desperately needed help from private aid organizations and the UN. But the Taliban resented the foreign presence and made it difficult for the NGOs to work. The Taliban leadership believed that the UN conspired against Afghanistan, preventing other countries from recognizing the regime. The UN had no authority to do such a thing. The suspicions were unfounded.

However, as funding for the private and UN charity agencies dropped off when information about the Taliban regime came out, several of the NGOs simply withdrew from the country. They were upset because the Taliban refused to let them continue to help women.

The Taliban ordered the heads of three separate UN agencies to leave the country. The UN High Commission for Refugees lodged a protest when a woman lawyer had been forced to interview Taliban

Internally displaced people and returning refugees wait outside a mobile clinic run by Relief International during the fighting that unsettled Afghanistan before the Taliban seized power in 1996. *(Photo by R. Colville/ United Nations)*

officials from behind a curtain. Save the Children pulled out of Afghanistan because the Taliban refused to allow them to include women in their classes giving instructions on how to identify and avoid land mines.

Other groups were suspected of attempting to spread Christianity and to convert Muslims. The Taliban had made it a serious crime to try to convert a Muslim to Christianity. They expelled several Christian-based charities on grounds of doing missionary work.

In September 1997, early in the Taliban regime, the police arrested Emma Bonino, who headed the European Commission for Humanitarian Affairs. She was held in prison along with 19 foreign journalists and aid workers for three hours before being released. They were jailed because as they were touring a hospital funded by the European Union some of the journalists photographed women patients in the ward. The Taliban expressly prohibited any photography of people at all.

Since the NGOs relied on both men and women employees from around the world, they ran into numerous severe problems. Some of the NGOs canceled their work in Afghanistan, closed their offices, and withdrew their personnel. Then, UN secretary-general Kofi Annan delivered an unusually harsh speech against the Taliban at the United Nations in 1997. By 2000, the UN pulled out its offices. The Taliban had cut itself off from the world.

WOMEN DURING THE TALIBAN REGIME

Traditional values among Muslims around the world are generally conservative regarding the relations between men and women. For example, in Saudi Arabia, women are not allowed to drive automobiles. Many Muslim societies expect women to wear a head scarf when appearing in public.

Even so, the specifics of the rules imposed by the Taliban were shocking to Muslims outside Afghanistan. Even those in very traditional Muslim societies found the ideas strange. During the Taliban regime, the treatment of women and girls attracted international attention and outrage.

Afghan women living abroad in the United States or Europe who had fled from the communist regime or from the war of the mujahideen against Soviet troops were horrified to learn what was going on in their homeland after the Taliban took over. They formed several international organizations and made their voices of protest heard. The facts that they uncovered and the reports that they published shocked the whole world.

The Taliban set up a special government department, the Ministry for the Promotion of Virtue and Suppression of Vice (PVSV), with its own religious police to enforce the rules. The dreaded PVSV made sure that the rules were obeyed. They carried whips and guns. They used them to deal out punishments on the spot to those they observed breaking the new rules. Some other countries, such as Saudi Arabia, had similar ministries or commissions. But the Taliban PVSV was much more severe than other vice-suppression authorities.

Some of the rules that applied to men as well as women were unique in the Muslim world: The Taliban allowed no sports (including traditional Afghan sports and games such as flying kites and playing chess).

They prohibited television and movies. Roving bands of PVSV militia would break into houses that had satellite dishes or TV antennas and destroy all the television equipment.

Even so, a flourishing and outlawed black market developed for replacement TVs. The Taliban prohibited photographs of any living things. They destroyed the cameras of visiting journalists if they took a picture of anyone. But the strictures or constraints on women were particularly difficult and much worse.

Reports from the countryside reflected worse abuses. In one area, Taloqan, Amnesty International reported on widespread kidnappings.

AFGHAN WOMEN BEFORE THE TALIBAN

From the 1950s through the 1990s, women in Afghanistan, particularly in the larger cities, among the upper classes, and those educated abroad, had made many steps toward modern life. For example, in 1959, Prime Minister Daoud Khan and other members of the government would appear in public with their wives and daughters. Those women appeared in public with no veils or head scarves at all.

In 1964, the constitution approved by King Zahir Shah announced legal equality for men and women. The constitution also indicated that secular, or government, law would apply instead of religious law. Furthermore, the constitution set up a democratic process for electing parliament.

In the parliament elected in 1965, four women were among those elected. During the last days of the monarchy and under the People's Democratic Party of Afghanistan (PDPA), public schools for girls were established.

Women made many advances during the last days of the monarchy and during the rule of the PDPA. Many women went abroad to receive higher education. Graduates returned as teachers, college professors, doctors, lawyers, and administrators. A woman became a news anchor on the national television station.

In the 1970s in Kabul and other cities, women began adopting Western styles of dress. By the time of the Soviet invasion in 1979, the Afghan government estimated that about half of all college students, government workers, and teachers were women.

ROOTS OF TALIBAN IDEAS ABOUT WOMEN

As noted in the last chapter, when the Taliban came to power, they brought with them a mixture of ideas. Some of those ideas were derived from the traditional Pashtun society in which most of them had been raised, Pashtunwali.

Those social values had been further influenced by exposure in the madrassas of Pakistan to the extremely conservative ideas of the Deobandi sect. Traditional Pashtunwali values held that women should obey their husbands and should not protest even when a husband beat his wife. The conservative views of the Deobandi supported this second-class status for women.

The fact that most of the recruits to the Taliban had been raised in refugee camps added several other features to the ideas of the Taliban. When the refugees fled to Pakistan, family groups were broken up. Village elders were no longer present to pass down knowledge of traditions. Often, children were left as orphans, as both parents would be killed or separated from their children during the fighting.

When the boys were rounded up to attend madrassas, those schools were all male. For this reason, many young boys spent years with virtually no contact with mothers, aunts, sisters, or any other women. Some

Amnesty International is a group that looks into charges of violations of human rights around the world. The organization heard reports that women from both Taloqan and from the Shomali plains area were loaded on trucks and taken for sale to Pakistan.

Some were reported sold to the Arab gulf states for the sex trade. During the slaughter of more than 5,000 civilians in Mazar-e Sharif in 1998, there were reports that hundreds of girls and women were seized and raped. Many of those women were never found.

The specific rules that the Taliban imposed on women affected all areas of their lives. They prohibited a woman from traveling in public without a male relative. Women in public could be punished for speaking loudly or for laughing loud enough to be overheard. Even more drastic rules prohibited all women from any paid employment and prohibited girls from attending school.

experts on the rise of the Taliban think that the cause of their oppressive attitude toward women resulted in part from living for years in a nearly all-male society.

Once the Taliban was driven from power by Operation Enduring Freedom, Afghan girls were once again allowed to attend schools such as this one, supported by the UN Children's Fund. *(Photo by Fardin Waez/United Nations)*

In one reported case, a single mother knew that her small daughter needed to see a doctor. The only clinic that she could go to lay many blocks away in Kabul. The mother had no male relative to accompany her in the street, but she decided to chance it and take her child to the clinic by herself. Although she went out in a burqa, one of the PVSV police nevertheless challenged her. She pretended to ignore him and hurried on with her child. He shot her on the spot. When confronted about his decision, the religious policeman offered no apology. It violated sharia, he said, for a woman to be seen on the street without a male relative.

The Taliban even prohibited homeschooling. Numerous homes where the religious police suspected schooling were broken up and the families punished. Apparently concerned that a woman might be observed in her home without a burqa, the Taliban passed another rule

THE BURQA

Perhaps the most famous and most noticed change concerned the rule about what women could wear in public. A decree passed in 1997 declared that any woman who appeared out of her home had to wear a burqa (also spelled burka), a loose garment that covered the woman from head to toe. It had a small screen over the eyes so the wearer could see out. Any woman caught wearing Western clothes would be immediately stopped and whipped by members of the PVSV. If a woman wearing a burqa had it cut too short so that her ankles showed, she could be stopped and beaten. Some poor women could not afford to buy a burqa or the cloth to make one. In order to go out of the house to buy food or for any other purpose, they ran the risk of being stopped and beaten. Although the burqa had been a common garment in some of the rural Pashtun areas, many women in the cities had never worn one. Such women highly resented the burqa rule. But they had to obey or face being beaten.

An Afghan woman, wearing a burqa, walks with a child along the side of a road in northern Afghanistan. *(Photo by Steve Evans/Used under Creative Commons license)*

that any home with windows facing the street that housed one or more women had to have the windows painted over in black.

These restrictions represented a personal setback in the liberties and freedom of individuals. But the rules had larger immediate and disastrous social impacts. Once all women were prevented from employment, all women doctors, nurses, teachers, bank tellers, and workers for aid agencies had to leave their jobs. They were immediately thrown into poverty. Since most of the teachers in elementary schools were women, many schools had to close.

Because of the immediate crisis in health care, the Taliban did allow women to work in some health care occupations. However, women doctors had to wear a burqa, which made it very difficult to examine women patients. Male doctors could only examine a woman if she were clothed in a burqa, and the rules prohibited any male doctor from touching a woman patient. In July 2000, the Taliban prohibited even the UN agencies and foreign aid agencies from employing any women, except for those in the health care fields.

Because of the years of fighting, many husbands and fathers had been killed. Aid agencies estimated that there were 30,000 widows in the city of Kabul. Since these women were prohibited from working, they were forced to sell off whatever they owned to keep from starving.

Many had to put on a burqa and take their children into the street to beg for food or money for the children. The PVSV temporarily shut down a World Food Program bakery that provided food to some of the starving families in August 2000 because the Taliban had heard that the bakery employed women.

The Taliban rules regarding health care made it very hard for most women, especially for widows, to get any health care at all. Since the rules prohibited any woman from visiting a male doctor unless accompanied by a male relative, that alone prevented thousands of women from going to a doctor. Rumors came out of Kabul that some hospitals ignored the rules and restrictions but at the risk of severe punishment. In all of Afghanistan, only one maternity hospital remained open.

The Taliban punished adultery by stoning the adulterer to death or inflicting 100 lashes in public. In September 2000, a man was stoned in public in Faryab Province. The woman with whom he committed adultery got a sentence of 100 lashes. Another woman who had reputedly arranged the adultery received the sentence of 39 lashes.

Foreign women were also arrested and punished if they violated the Taliban version of sharia. The PVSV jailed a woman aid worker in July 2000 for promoting a system of home-based work and homeschooling for girls. After her release, the government expelled her from the country.

Women were not allowed to take a taxi unless they were accompanied by a male relative. In June 2000, the PVSV arrested four women who worked for the UN World Food Program because they did not have a male relative with them. Special city buses were set aside for women only. But the male drivers had to have a screen or curtain placed so they could not observe the women passengers.

The bus company provided only a limited number of women-designated buses, so women would have to wait extended periods for a bus. The bus drivers were not allowed to collect the fares from women. Boys under the age of 15 had to be used as fare collectors.

At first, the official response of the U.S. government to the Taliban had been very positive. President Bill Clinton and his secretary of state, Madeleine Albright, believed that the Taliban would help bring peace and stability to Afghanistan. Many people in the United States, in Europe, and in Afghanistan itself shared that hope.

However, as news came out of the country about the actual way in which the Taliban applied their version of sharia, public opinion forced the U.S. government to change its position. Even though they were prohibited from taking photographs or movies, foreign journalists got their stories out, describing the public executions, the thousands

These beggars in Kabul reflect the fact that Afghanistan is still a nation with countless unemployed, poor, and disabled people. In particular, many Afghan widows are forced to use their children to elicit contributions. *(Photo by Lizette Potgieter/Shutterstock)*

TELEVISION AND HOLLYWOOD JOIN THE CAUSE

Three hundred women's groups and labor organizations in the United States developed a signature campaign to gather support for Afghan women. Mavis Leno, the wife of the comedian Jay Leno, personally pledged $100,000 to the program. With support from Hollywood actors who met right after the 1999 Academy Awards ceremony, the issue of the Taliban treatment of Afghan women became a major popular cause.

Women's organizations that were powerful in the Democratic Party brought pressure to drop support of the Taliban. With public announcements from television and Hollywood personalities, more and more people took up the cause of women in Afghanistan.

of women and children begging for food, and numerous incidents of beatings on the streets.

As the movement of support for Afghan women grew, the government heard the protests. Hillary Clinton, the wife of President Bill Clinton, was working on building her own political base with the support of women's organizations. She joined the chorus of those critical of the Taliban and made many statements condemning the Taliban. People knew she spoke not only for herself but for the administration.

Secretary of State Madeleine Albright also made it clear that the United States no longer supported the Taliban regime. Only Saudi Arabia, the United Arab Emirates, and Pakistan gave the Taliban official recognition by sending diplomats to Afghanistan.

Of course, the problems in Afghanistan were not confined to the treatment of women. Afghanistan continued to face other crises. Factions fought a brutal civil war. The government suppressed all dissent. The country was among the poorest in the world. Opium poppy cultivation spread. The country was devastated from years of war. Men were forced to wear beards and a traditional hat. But the issue of women's rights abuse appeared to arouse American public opinion more than the other crimes of the regime.

9/11 AND AFGHANISTAN

The event that led to U.S. troops and those of allied countries to invade and occupy Afghanistan was the hijacking of four commercial airplanes on September 11, 2001. Known forevermore, as the 9/11 attacks, the hijackings led to the deaths of nearly 3,000 Americans and foreign residents in the United States.

The carefully planned and coordinated attacks were the worst terrorist acts in modern history. Planned and financed by Osama bin Laden's organization, they were carried off by a group of 20 young recruits.

Their plan was to simultaneously hijack four aircraft. Fully loaded with fuel, two of the aircraft were supposed to crash into the two tallest buildings in New York City, the World Trade Center (WTC) towers. Another was to crash into the Pentagon. The terrorists planned to take the fourth aircraft and crash it into either the White House or the U.S. Capitol building in Washington, D.C.

The four hijacked aircraft were:

American Flight 11, Boston to Los Angeles. It crashed into the North Tower of the WTC at 8:46 A.M.

United Flight 175, Boston to Los Angeles. It crashed into the South Tower of the WTC at 9:03 A.M.

American Flight 75, Washington Dulles to Los Angeles. It crashed into the Pentagon at 9:37 A.M.

United Flight 93, Newark to San Francisco. It crashed into a field near Shanksville, Pennsylvania, at 10:02 A.M., after passengers rushed the hijacker-controlled cockpit. Although all aboard the plane died, the passengers' heroic effort saved hundreds more lives at the Washington target of the hijackers.

A New York City firefighter looks up at what remains of the World Trade Center towers after the terrorist attacks of September 11, 2001. It was this incident that led to the invasion of Afghanistan that October. *(U.S. Navy)*

During the takeover of the airplanes, as flight attendants and passengers called authorities, friends, colleagues, and relatives from the hijacked planes, they could identify the hijackers by the seats they

A section of the Pentagon lies in ruins during the night of September 11, 2001, after terrorists crashed an airliner into the building. *(U.S. Navy)*

had been assigned. The seat reservations showed the identity of all of the hijackers. Among each of the hijacking groups, one hijacker had received at least some training in flying commercial airplanes. The others were there to provide muscle, to overcome the aircraft officers and flight attendants and to control the passengers.

To frighten the passengers, the hijackers claimed to have bombs, but there was no evidence that they really had any. They used box cutters that they had smuggled aboard to intimidate or kill those who tried to stop them. Aboard the four planes, they killed several passengers, flight attendants, and airplane pilots so that they could take over the aircraft and fly them toward their targets.

The two aircraft that struck the World Trade Center towers caused the vast majority of the deaths that resulted from the attacks. Hundreds of office and restaurant workers on floors above the impact zone were trapped. Some in the buildings tried to escape to the roof to await evacuation by helicopter. However, the doors to the roofs were locked and could not be unlocked. When each of the towers collapsed, all of the hundreds of people trapped above the impact zones were killed.

As fires raged through the buildings, some attempted to escape by taking the elevators. Several of the elevator cars stalled. Some of the people in them never escaped. Others tried to go down the emergency stairwells, but smoke, darkness, and confusion about the doorways in the stairs left many trapped.

Some, rather than face death from raging fires and smoke, broke the windows and jumped to their deaths. Falling bodies sometimes struck rescue workers and others evacuating from the ground floor, killing some of the people on the sidewalks nearby.

Since New York is a television and media center, the fires and collapse of the WTC towers were broadcast live. As tens of thousands of office workers and residents fled from downtown with its smoke and dust, some left on foot across bridges and some aboard dozens of ferries. The nation and the world were stunned and shocked.

Not counting the hijackers, 2,973 people had been killed, the greatest loss in U.S. history as a result of a hostile attack on the country. Of those killed, 343 were members of the New York Fire Department who were trying to rescue others. The New York Port Authority lost 37 policemen. The New York Police Department lost another 23. These were the first- and second-largest number of U.S. policemen ever killed in a single event. Several hundred of the victims were foreigners resident in the United States, including British citizens and also many Muslims from various countries.

At the Pentagon, the loss of human life was far smaller. In addition to the 64 people aboard American Flight 75, 125 people inside the building were killed. Because the structure is not a skyscraper and the

THE WORLD TRADE CENTER AND THE EARLIER BOMBING

The World Trade Center was designed by the architect Minoru Yamasaki, and construction began in 1966. Both towers of the center were 110 stories tall and built over an existing subway. As part of the deal to build the structure, the Port Authority of New York and New Jersey took over the rail line, and it became the Port Authority Transit–Hudson, or PATH. Many PATH policemen would assist in the effort to rescue and evacuate the buildings during the attack.

The North Tower was completed in December 1970. The South Tower was finished in July 1971. Altogether the buildings of the WTC contained 13.4 million square feet of offices. On the 106th and 107th floors of the North Tower was the Windows on the World restaurant. Other buildings in the complex included the Marriott World Trade Center and lower-rise buildings numbers 6 and 7 that housed government and private offices.

On February 26, 1993, a truck containing a bomb was detonated in the North Tower parking basement, leading to the evacuation of the center. The intent had been to topple the North Tower into the South Tower. The structures did not fall in the 1993 attack, but six people were killed and over 1,000 were injured. Several of those who had planned and carried out the bomb attack were later arrested and convicted of planting the bomb. Although not members of al-Qaeda, they were a group of jihadists with similar ideas. They were led by Omar Abdel-Rahman, a blind Egyptian cleric traveling on a Sudanese passport.

fire was soon contained, evacuation and rescue work went much better. Furthermore, the various emergency response teams in the northern Virginia area around the Pentagon had practiced coordinated efforts. They were able to quickly provide ambulances, fire equipment, and other help.

The attacks had struck not only at human lives but at the symbols of American power: its major position in world commerce and its military headquarters. If the fourth plane had hit its target of the White House or the Capitol, a central structure symbolizing American government power would also have been the scene of further tragedy.

The crew of the USS *Cole* escort their wounded ship aboard a U.S. Navy tug vessel in the harbor of Aden, Yemen. On October 12, 2000, al-Qaeda terrorists had exploded a small boat against the side of the *Cole,* killing 19 U.S. sailors. *(Department of Defense)*

Although bin Laden had issued his fatwa against the United States in 1998, the American public had learned very little about him and al-Qaeda over the next three years. Investigations by the FBI into the attack on the USS *Cole* that had taken the lives of 17 sailors and injured others and the embassy bombings in Africa had revealed that al-Qaeda was also behind those bombings.

Evidence gathered before 9/11 from intercepted phone messages and other sources indicated to U.S. intelligence agencies that al-Qaeda planned still another attack inside the United States. In particular, many experts had feared that another al-Qaeda attack of some kind would come on January 1, 2000. In fact, a terrorist was arrested at the Canadian-U.S. border when he tried to bring in explosives that he planned to set off at the Los Angeles International Airport on New Year's Day.

Later investigation revealed that aspects of the 9/11 planning and the plot had been turned up by different agencies, including the CIA and the FBI. But because of rules and practices that prohibited sharing

ATTACK ON THE USS *COLE*

On October 12, 2000, in the harbor of Aden, Yemen, at 11:15 A.M. as the USS *Cole* prepared to leave port, a small fiberglass boat pulled alongside. Two men aboard the small boat brought it to a stop near the middle of the *Cole.* Inside the U.S. destroyer, some sailors were having lunch, while others were standing watch. The two men aboard the small fishing craft stood, waved, and then remained standing. An enormous explosion blasted a 40-foot hole in the hull of the ship, killing 17 sailors and injuring 39 more. The blast was so powerful it knocked over cars ashore, and people several miles away thought they had felt an earthquake.

Investigation by FBI agents in Yemen was difficult, but eventually, with the cooperation of Yemeni authorities, several of the conspirators who had bought the explosives and planned the attack were arrested. Although it soon became obvious that the planners and financial backers of the attack were al-Qaeda and Osama bin Laden, the Clinton administration decided not to launch a missile retaliation.

The damaged *Cole* was eventually loaded aboard a huge transport vessel and shipped back to the United States where it was fully repaired. As late as nine years later, families of the sailors who were killed asked why the perpetrators of the crime had never been brought to trial. One of the reasons was that evidence against them had been gathered when they were held in military custody, without attorneys present. So any case against them in a U.S. criminal court would be immediately dismissed.

such information, U.S. government agencies were unprepared for what happened.

Of course it was hard to prepare for such an event. Never before had hijackers taken over an aircraft and then made it serve as a missile. There had never been a hijacking of several American aircraft at the same time.

Immediately after the attack, as surveillance camera tapes and airline reservations were checked against seat numbers, the identity of the 19 hijackers and their connections to al-Qaeda became clear. (One of the 20 recruits to the plan was unable to join the attack.) Within days, U.S. officials realized that the attack had been planned and carried out by terrorists arranged and funded by al-Qaeda.

American counterterrorist specialists knew that al-Qaeda had its bases in Afghanistan. They also knew that the Taliban government had been providing facilities to bin Laden since 1996. Investigators soon learned that the hijackers who had piloted the planes had taken courses at American air-training schools. Some suspicions had been raised about them while they were attending the schools. Even so, none of them had been arrested or questioned by authorities.

In Afghanistan, as live television pictures of the attacks were broadcast, bin Laden was meeting with his lieutenants. Some of them knew the attacks were coming, but most of them did not know the details. They cheered the news of the first collision with the South Tower of the WTC. Then bin Laden told them to wait and held up one finger. At the second collision, he again said to wait, holding up two fingers.

It was clear to his associates that bin Laden had helped in the planning and funding of the attacks. Later investigation revealed that he had channeled between $400,000 and $500,000 to the hijackers to finance their training, travel, housing, and other details of the attacks.

As the horror of the attacks sank in, Americans compared them to the Japanese attack on Pearl Harbor. Most of those lost in that December 7, 1941, attack had been sailors and other military personnel. The attack had been launched to cripple America's ability to fight.

The 9/11 attacks were more horrifying and evil than the Pearl Harbor attack for a number of reasons. The victims had been innocent Americans and foreign nationals, engaged in ordinary business. Only a handful, in the Pentagon, had been part of the military establishment. The Japanese attack in 1941 had been a military attack on a military target. The 9/11 attacks were a case of mass murder on an unprecedented scale.

Americans responded with an outburst of patriotism. Hundreds of thousands of Americans flew American flags at their homes or on their cars or hung them from overpasses across highways and freeways. Others posted pictures at the site of the World Trade Center of missing or killed loved ones or left candles, flowers, and other memorials to the victims.

Immediately after the attacks, on September 12, the 19 member nations of the North Atlantic Treaty Organization (NATO) had voted to treat the attacks on the United States as an attack on each of them if it was proven the attacks had come from a foreign source. Under that treaty, they committed to provide military assistance to the attacked country. On October 2, 2001, the NATO members would restate their commitment, since by then it had become clear that the attacks indeed had come from a foreign source.

CRIME OR ACT OF WAR?

The attacks on the World Trade Center and Pentagon could be viewed either as a criminal act or as an act of war, or as both. Clearly, the 19 hijackers and those who planned and funded the attacks were engaged in a criminal conspiracy, resulting in the murder of 2,973 people, most of whom were U.S. citizens. They had destroyed hundreds of millions of dollars of private and public property. Under the laws of every country in the world such actions would be considered felonies. In many countries including the United States, the punishment for criminal conspiracy to commit murder would be death.

However, the scale of the attacks was so great that it also seemed to be an act of war. When it is remembered that the United States entered World War II because of the Japanese attack on Pearl Harbor, Hawaii, that killed 2,400 people, the 9/11 attacks seemed just as, or more, serious. Clearly, the hijackers had intended to strike at U.S. civilians and at U.S. buildings that were central to America's place in business and world affairs. But usually a war is launched by a country against another country, and al-Qaeda was an international organization, not a government of a country.

President George W. Bush's immediate reaction was to say, "This is war." His response was to mobilize the military, to demand the Afghanistan Taliban government yield up Osama bin Laden and his lieutenants, and then to attack the Afghanistan government when it failed to surrender the culprits. Although the Taliban had not been involved in planning or funding the attacks, the majority of Americans supported

This was the first time in the 50-year history of NATO that it invoked Article V, the article that provided for joint military aid if a member was attacked. Australia also promised military support under the separate ANZUS treaty on the same grounds, treating the attack on the United States as an act of war against Australia.

On Monday, September 17, 2001, the Pakistani government, acting under pressure from the United States, sent an ultimatum to the Afghanistan government of the Taliban. The message was delivered by Pakistani diplomats. Pakistan was one of the very few governments with diplomats in Afghanistan. The message said that the Taliban should immediately surrender Osama bin Laden and members of his organization or face a devastating reprisal by the United States and its allies.

treating the attack on Afghanistan as part of a larger "war on terror," rather than as an attempt to catch and prosecute a group of criminals.

Later, as the war in Afghanistan lengthened, people debated whether it was right to treat the hijackings as a crime or an act of war.

President George W. Bush is applauded after his address at the Pentagon memorial service on October 11, 2001, in honor of those who perished in the terrorist attack of September 11. *(Department of Defense)*

Meanwhile, the U.S. secretary of state Colin Powell announced on CNN that if the Taliban did not expel bin Laden and turn him over to the United States, they would be held accountable for the help they had provided him. They would either help "rip up the organization" or they would "suffer the full wrath of the United States and other countries."

On September 21, 2001, President Bush personally announced the ultimatum to the Taliban leadership, spelling out the details of the demand. The Taliban were told that they had to close every terrorist training camp in Afghanistan. They also had to provide access so that the United States could be sure that no camps still operated. Further, they had to hand over every member of al-Qaeda in the country. Meanwhile, the religious leaders of Afghanistan called for an investigation, but Mullah Omar, the emir of Afghanistan, went into hiding.

Omar found it difficult to surrender bin Laden for several reasons. The Taliban relied at this point on some $20 million per year funneled to the government from contributions collected by al-Qaeda. Also, the Pashtunwali code required a host to protect a guest, even if the guest broke the law. Furthermore, Mullah Omar apparently realized that if he surrendered bin Laden to the United States, he would lose credibility among his strongly anti-American and radical Taliban followers.

Diplomats and observers concluded that the Taliban were stalling. So the United States rapidly prepared its military plans. U.S. military officials worked with allies to coordinate the next step. In a coordinated effort, U.S. and Coalition forces began an invasion of Afghanistan on October 7, 2001, less than a month after the attack on the United States. This was the beginning of Operation Enduring Freedom, in which U.S. forces would begin the hunt for Osama bin Laden and assist in the liberation of Afghanistan from the rule of the Taliban.

AMERICANS AT WAR

October–December 2001

Right after the 9/11 attacks on the World Trade Center and the Pentagon, U.S. officials began getting ready for a possible assault on Afghanistan. Meanwhile, local resistance armies in Afghanistan that had fought against the Taliban regime drew hope from the idea that the United States might come to their aid.

In Brussels, Belgium, even before President Bush asked Congress for authority to launch an attack, NATO leaders voted to help the United States in a military action if it was proven that the attacks on America came from a foreign source. On September 12, the UN Security Council passed resolution 1368 that condemned the terrorist attacks on the United States. The Council also asked all governments to help in rooting out terrorist organizations. Although NATO forces operated under a joint command, U.S. forces operated under direct U.S. command.

On September 14, the U.S. Congress approved the use of military force in Afghanistan. The vote was 420 votes to 1 in the House of Representatives. It was 98 to 0 in the Senate. American forces were already beginning their operations and planning for more.

When Mullah Omar and the Taliban leadership refused to give up Osama bin Laden, U.S. aircraft began a selected bombing attack on Afghanistan. At the same time, the forces of the Northern Alliance began moving.

A limited number of U.S. Special Forces were secretly dropped into Afghanistan to assist the Northern Alliance in mid-September. At first, the United States did not want to appear to be invading the country and wanted to rely as much as possible on Afghan forces to lead in the attack on the Taliban. As it turned out, the defeat of the Taliban regime came so quickly that very few American troops had to take part in their

This propaganda poster promoting Osama bin Laden and his cause was found by members of a U.S. Navy SEAL team at a site in eastern Afghanistan where they were seeking intelligence information that might help to track down bin Laden. (*Department of Defense*)

defeat. Most of the few dozen Special Forces troops were employed in using laser devices to mark targets for aircraft attack.

As early as September 13, two days after the attacks on the WTC and the Pentagon, the CIA also flew a small team into Afghanistan. They took the assignment to work with the Northern Alliance. However, Operation Enduring Freedom did not officially begin until October 7, and the British announced their support with Operation Veritas on October 16.

Until October 19, when more forces began to arrive, only a very limited number of U.S. Special Forces and CIA personnel were in Afghanistan. However, U.S. aircraft staged many missions in the period from October 7 through December 4, hitting terrorist and Taliban centers. They also dropped leaflets, food, medicine, and clothes.

Some reports indicated that the United States had as few as 10 men on the ground before October 19. On October 19, more than 100 Army Rangers parachuted into an air base outside of Kandahar. In another raid, a group of Army Rangers and Delta Force raided a house sometimes used by Mullah Omar, but he had already left.

The Northern Alliance captured the town of Mazar-e Sharif on November 9. Remembering the holocaust that had occurred there in 1998 when the Taliban had killed more than 5,000 civilians, U.S. leaders feared that there might be retaliation against Taliban supporters

THE NORTHERN ALLIANCE

The Northern Alliance was formally called the United Islamic Front for the Salvation of Afghanistan, or United Front. It drew on three ethnic-based armies largely made up of troops from the non-Pashtun regions of the north. The Uzbek leader, Abdul Rashid Dostum, had a reputation for betraying his alliances, but his supporters claimed those rumors were false.

The Northern Alliance armies had been part of the mujahideen resistance to the Soviets, organized in one of the Pakistan-based political parties, the Islamic Society, Jamiat-i-Islami (JIA). It had been founded by the Tajik leader Burhanuddin Rabbani.

The Tajik army was commanded by Ahmad Shah Massoud until he was assassinated by agents from al-Qaeda on September 9, 2001. Massoud was replaced by General Ustad Atta Mohammed. The third commander was the Hazara general Mohammad Mohaqiq. The Northern Alliance had a series of rapid victories in the 2001 defeat of the Taliban, conquering the city of Mazar-e Sharif on November 9 and then chasing the Taliban out of the capital, Kabul, on November 13.

Taking a break here are troops under the command of Afghan General Rashid Dostum, one of the prominent leaders of the Northern Alliance that joined the U.S. and NATO forces in overthrowing the Taliban in fall 2001. *(Department of Defense)*

for those earlier atrocities. However, the Taliban withdrew as Northern Alliance armies under the leadership of the mujahideen general Dostum freed the city.

B-52 bombers blasted out Taliban defenders in a gorge to the south of Mazar-e Sharif and also hit a nearby pass controlled by Taliban defenders. The Taliban fired antiaircraft guns at the bombers, without effect. The Northern Alliance troops under Dostum finally moved across the Pul-i-Imam Bukhri Bridge and took the main military base and airport.

The Taliban pulled back 12,000 of their own troops and a reported 2,000 foreign fighters supporting them. These volunteers came from Saudi Arabia, Chechnya, and Pakistan, among other countries. The Taliban and their foreign volunteers left in pickup trucks and stolen SUVs, driving north and east to Kudzu in their retreat.

While the city of Mazar-e Sharif was under attack, a group of about 900 young Pakistani volunteers, newly recruited from madrassas, arrived to help the Taliban. They gathered in a former girls' school. As the Northern Alliance approached, the volunteers tried to negotiate a surrender. Outside observers are not sure what happened next. Either U.S. bombs or Northern Alliance heavy gunfire hit the school. An estimated 800 of the Pakistani Taliban died, either from explosions or shot by Northern Alliance troops. The claims and counterclaims were never resolved.

In late November, one of the strangest episodes of the Afghanistan War occurred at Qala-i-Jangi, a fortress/prison on the outskirts of Mazar-e Sharif. At least 300 suspected Taliban fighters were being held there by Northern Alliance forces, when on November 25 a CIA agent was brutally killed while trying to interrogate some of the prisoners. A prison uprising then erupted, and it was December 1 before Northern Alliance, U.S., and British forces finally took control of the fortress. Only some 80 Taliban survived, among them a young American, John Walker Lindh. He had grown up in Marin County, California, and gone to Afghanistan where, after attending a madrassa to study the Quran, he joined the Taliban. In October 2002, he would plead guilty in an American court and be sentenced to 20 years in prison.

After the capture of the northeast city of Mazar-e Sharif and its airport, 1,000 U.S. 10th Mountain Rangers flew in to hold the airport. This airport provided the first U.S.-captured air base inside Afghanistan, where U.S. supplies and soldiers could be landed directly in the country. U.S. and British forces were soon taking over more air bases.

U.S. Army Special Operations Forces personnel load their all-terrain vehicles and equipment onto a Chinook helicopter at Bagram Air Base during Operation Enduring Freedom. *(Department of Defense)*

During the 2001 invasion and expulsion of the Taliban, the Bagram Air Base, 27 miles north of Kabul, was first captured by a team from the British Special Boat Service, the British Royal Navy's Special Forces unit. By December, troops from the U.S. 10th Mountain Division and from the Special Operations Command shared the base with the British force.

The U.K. force also included Bravo and Charlie Companies of the 40 Commando Royal Marines, based in Somerset, England. Later, U.S. troops from the 10th Mountain Division provided patrols and perimeter guards. The first large deployments of U.S. troops were put through Bagram Air Base. More came through the Kandahar airport. Local workers and U.S., Italian, and Polish troops repaired the runways.

Later, the Bagram Air Base included a detention facility where captured members of al-Qaeda were held and questioned. Representatives of the International Red Cross visited the facility every two weeks. Even so, the detention facility became controversial because of reputed harsh methods of questioning.

As the Northern Alliance troops advanced north of Kabul, the Taliban units began to surrender, retreat, or sometimes join in large groups with the Northern Alliance. Following air strikes from U.S.

B-52 bombers and a two-hour artillery attack by the Northern Alliance, the Taliban lines fell apart in early November. As they fled from Kabul, armored units of the Northern Alliance Guards Brigade advanced, together with long lines of foot soldiers, capturing Taliban equipment.

By the evening of November 12, Northern Alliance troops crossed the Shomali Plain and reached Qarabagh. They ran into only scattered resistance from the Taliban rearguard. Most of the Northern Alliance troops halted at the Khairkhanah Pass. Civilians from the freed city of Kabul rushed out to greet the Northern Alliance liberators. Some of the greeters came in taxis.

The next morning, Northern Alliance troops and hastily organized volunteers started to police the city to prevent looting. Even so, mobs of Kabul townsmen tracked down and killed remaining Pakistani and Arab Taliban soldiers. In the Shahre Nao Park, a mob beat and shot to death three Pakistanis, chanting "Death to Pakistan!"

A military and security council, headed by the Northern Alliance defense minister, General Mohammad Fahim, worked to establish order. After the fall of Mazar-e Sharif and Kabul, the defeat of the Taliban came very quickly. Whole Taliban units either surrendered or switched sides to join the Northern Alliance forces. Afghan Taliban were sometimes accepted into Northern Alliance units. But the Northern Alliance tended to hunt down and shoot the foreign Taliban fighters.

The quick victories by the Northern Alliance armies caused some optimism among U.S. authorities. However, the main armies were Tajik, Uzbek, and Hazara. That created the possibility that the Pashtun areas of southern Afghanistan would resent any new leadership that came after the Taliban were defeated. To ensure support among the Pashtun, some of the anti-Taliban leaders had to come from the Pashtun ethnic group.

Two Pashtun leaders who had been living outside Afghanistan, Hamid Karzai and Gul Agha Sherzai, had returned to the country to gather their followers and lead them against the Taliban. Karzai had been a deputy foreign minister in the 1990s government overthrown by the Taliban. Sherzai had been the governor of Kandahar before the Taliban took over. Karzai and Sherzai had been organizing forces north and south of the city of Kandahar, the center of Taliban support.

Karzai soon won some victories helped by a small U.S. Special Forces team. Special Forces Operational Detachment Alpha (ODA)

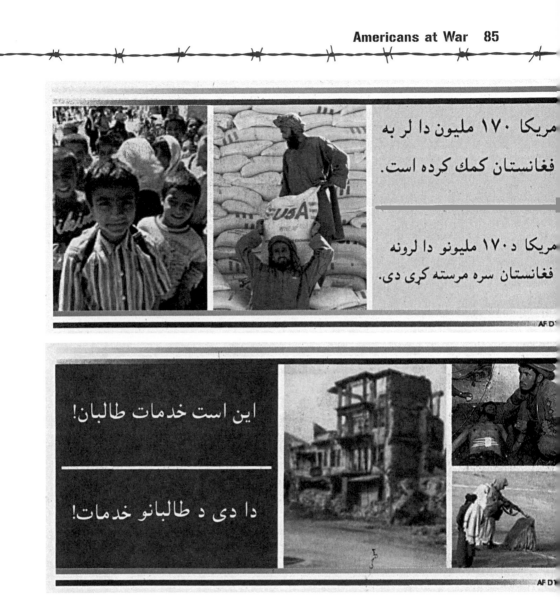

Illustrated leaflets such as these were air-dropped over Afghanistan during the opening phase of Operation Enduring Freedom. Written in Afghan languages, one side pictured atrocities committed by the Taliban *(bottom)* and the other side showed Afghans unloading bags of food labeled "USA." *(Library of Congress)*

574 was a group of 11 men headed by Captain Jason Amerine. After Karzai's forces took the town of Tarin Kowt, about 70 miles north of Kandahar, the Taliban decided to attack his base. They sent about 80 trucks and cars and some 500 troops to drive him out.

Captain Amerine set up his laser range-finding equipment on a ridge that looked out over the road approaching the town. When the Taliban group of trucks came in view, he guided a bomb fired from a Navy F-14 Tomcat right into the front of a truck. The resulting explosion blew up the truck, its antiaircraft gun, and all aboard. One by one, Amerine's men were able to continue to target the Taliban trucks in the convoy.

Karzai's force drove off a group of Taliban on foot. Bombs from Amerine's team harassed the retreating Taliban. All in all, an estimated 300 Taliban were killed. The bombs wrecked 30 vehicles. With this good news, Karzai led his offensive into Kandahar, adding to his credibility. The system of U.S. support seemed to work.

Meanwhile, Osama bin Laden and the al-Qaeda leadership had retreated to a complex of caves and tunnels that bin Laden had built in the Tora Bora region. Northern Alliance troops with a small number of U.S. Special Forces moved on the hideout from three sides. However, the fourth side faced toward Pakistan.

DAISY CUTTER

In trying to dislodge al-Qaeda from the deep cave and tunnel complex in Tora Bora, the United States used the largest nonnuclear bomb ever used in warfare, the Daisy Cutter. Officially known as BLU-82, and sometimes called Big Blue 82, the bomb weighed 15,000 pounds. It had been used in the Vietnam War to clear areas of the jungle so that helicopters could land. The name "Daisy Cutter" came from the fuse assembly that allowed for the weapon to be detonated a few feet above the ground to ensure that the maximum amount of vegetation would be cleared.

The bomb was not dropped from a bomber aircraft but from the cargo-carrying 130H Hercules. The bomb spread out an explosive slurry mix of ammonium nitrate and aluminum particles that then detonated. The explosives made up 12,600 pounds of the weapon. The weapon destroyed everything in an area about 3,600 feet in diameter. It sent a shock wave that could be felt for miles. The mushroom cloud from the explosion resembled that from a small atomic bomb. The blast was so extensive that the plane dropping it had to be at least 6,000 feet above the point of detonation.

The bomb cost about $27,000. It was about five feet in diameter and about 17 feet long, the size of a small car. The Department of Defense announced that four Daisy Cutters had been dropped in Afghanistan by December 13, 2001.

By the end of November, the Northern Alliance had gathered a force of about 2,500 troops near the Tora Bora hideout of al-Qaeda. They had several Russian tanks left behind by the Soviets 12 years earlier. The Taliban and al-Qaeda forces retreated up into the rugged mountain region with snow-covered valleys, forests, and a cave complex. As the Northern Alliances forces closed in from three sides, U.S. aircraft dropped heavy weapons, including the 15,000-pound Daisy Cutter, on the suspected al-Qaeda positions.

When troops finally advanced into the caves, they found stores of equipment and ammunition left behind by the retreating Taliban and al-Qaeda forces. At first, rumors circulated that bin Laden had been killed in the bombing. Later, however, it became clear that he and his followers had escaped into Pakistan. Some reporters picked up stories that some Northern Alliance officers had taken bribes to let bin Laden

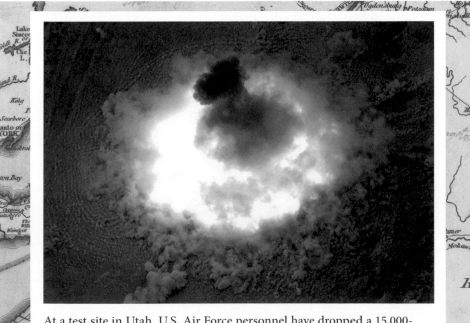

At a test site in Utah, U.S. Air Force personnel have dropped a 15,000-pound bomb to determine its effectiveness and impact. Known as the Daisy Cutter, this was the most powerful nonnuclear explosive in the U.S. arsenal and was used primarily in Afghanistan to blast caves and tunnels where al-Qaeda or Taliban members were believed to be hiding. *(U.S. Air Force)*

A JUST WAR?

Thinkers on international law since St. Augustine (354–430) and St. Thomas Aquinas (1225–74) have developed seven principles or considerations to determine whether a war is "just" or legitimate. Those in favor and those against the war in Afghanistan have debated each of the principles.

1. A just war must be authorized by a legitimate authority.

    Proponents: President Bush had approval from Congress under the War Powers Act. UN Security Council resolution 1386 passed on December 20, 2001, and provided further legitimacy.

    Opponents: The 9/11 act was a crime, not an act of war. The War Powers Act itself may be unconstitutional. U.S. forces did not act under the UN mandate until 2006.

2. A just war can only be fought if it is started with right intentions, such as to redress a wrong.

    Proponents: The attack on Afghanistan was justified by 9/11.

    Opponents: Afghans were not the criminals behind 9/11.

3. A just war can only be fought if there is a reasonable chance of success.

    Proponents: The quick victory over the Taliban demonstrated that there was sufficient chance of success; U.S., Coalition, and Northern Alliance forces were more than enough to defeat Afghanistan's Taliban army.

    Opponents: Bush deflected U.S. troops from full defeat of the Taliban because he held them back for use in Iraq, reducing chances for success. Also, historically, Afghanistan defeated both the British Empire and the Soviet army. The extended war demonstrates the chances for success were very poor.

and his group escape, and the failure to capture or kill him became a lasting controversy, both in Afghanistan and in the United States.

The quick victory over the Taliban was gratifying to the U.S. authorities and public. However, it left many questions unanswered. Heated, politically loaded debates and arguments sprang up, trying to assign blame for the escape of bin Laden. Since the Taliban were not

4. The damage of the war must be proportional to the injury suffered.

Proponents: The United States committed minimum troops; battles were swift; and the attacks of 9/11 were a devastating blow to the United States.

Opponents: The Daisy Cutters and other U.S. weapons were not needed; the number of casualties in Afghanistan since 2001 is many times more than those suffered by the United States.

5. A just war should be waged only as a last resort.

Proponents: An ultimatum was delivered and rejected by Mullah Omar, the leader of the Taliban.

Opponents: Omar might have turned over bin Laden eventually; diplomacy might have worked better but was not tried in the heat of anger over 9/11.

6. The real reason for the war should show right intent and should be the stated reason.

Proponents: The real and stated reason for the war was to apprehend al-Qaeda leadership and remove the Taliban from power.

Opponents: The war was part of President George W. Bush's plan to export Western-style democracy to countries in the region that were unsuited to that form of government.

7. The goal of a just war should be to reestablish peace. The peace after the war should be better than the peace that would exist if the war had not been fought.

Proponents: By forcing bin Laden into hiding, there has been a good peace; the United States did not suffer another attack during the George Bush administration.

Opponents: Afghanistan has suffered from continuing conflict; peace has not been reestablished in eight years. Furthermore, bin Laden remains at large.

part of the new interim government, they would continue to resist it. As in many U.S. wars, the public and politicians debated whether or not the U.S. forces in Afghanistan were engaged in a justified war.

Congress had almost unanimously approved the use of force to invade Afghanistan and pursue bin Laden. Among the 421 members of Congress and 98 senators, there had been only one vote against the

A British army officer coordinates his vehicles at a security stop in Helmand Province, preparatory to moving a new turbine from the Kandahar airfield to a dam in the region. *(Department of Defense)*

decision. Yet the war in Afghanistan, like other U.S. wars, soon became the subject of disagreement. Not only did Americans question whether the war itself was justified, but they asked if it was being fought well.

Even so, defenders of the war pointed out that the Taliban had been defeated with very few American casualties. In the year 2001, only 12 American military personnel were killed in Afghanistan, and in 2002, only another 49 died in military action. The war, as had been planned, had been largely a military operation of the Northern Alliance, with aid from the United States and other NATO members.

Many Americans asked why U.S. troops had not been committed in larger numbers. Later, after the United States invaded Iraq in 2003, some accused the Bush administration of planning that attack early and withholding troops from Afghanistan to be able to have them available for Iraq.

Whatever the reasoning behind such arguments, the international efforts to bring peace to Afghanistan and the U.S. role in that work would continue for many years.

OCCUPATION AND INTERNATIONAL FORCES

As U.S. forces helped the Northern Alliance win a quick victory over the Taliban, some NATO nations and other U.S. allies made good on their promises to help. Soon after U.S. troops began to arrive in 2001, troops from Britain, Australia, Canada, Germany, the Netherlands, and other countries came to help.

British Special Forces troops, like those of the U.S. forces, at first came in quite small numbers to help liberate specific points. Like the United States, Britain wanted to make sure that the defeat of the Taliban was seen as a victory by Afghans, not the result of a foreign invasion.

U.S. forces were confused by Afghan methods of warfare. The Afghans relied on negotiation and sometime switched allegiances to cut back the number of casualties. Officers and troops in the Afghan units on opposite sides often knew each other personally. They were sometimes members of the same family. They would talk to each other during the battles. Radio messages included not only warnings and insults but sometimes family news. Often the radio talk was not coded. Both sides could hear clear directions about bringing in artillery fire or movements of troops.

After exchanges of bluffs and threats, sometimes one side would make the other side believe it had no chance. Then the local field officers would arrange a quiet surrender and cease-fire. Often surrender simply meant that the side that thought it was weaker would walk away from the battle. Sometimes the losers threw away their weapons and melted into the general population. Although this method might reduce bloodshed, it left the U.S. advisers and troops puzzled.

When a large group surrendered to their fellow Afghans, they would often not be searched for weapons. Sometimes, after a few days, the losers would show up with their weapons to join the side of the winners. Even though the Afghans would sometimes commit terrible atrocities and retaliate against captured prisoners, at other times a battle could end with a discussion and a quiet surrender of territory. However, while Afghans often worked things out in this friendly way, foreign fighters and al-Qaeda fighters did not play by the same rules.

In the city of Kunduz, some hard-core fighters shot Northern Alliance officers who were coming forward to accept a previously arranged surrender. And at Mazar-e Sharif, Pakistanis killed 12 mullahs who had been sent to arrange terms of surrender. In November 2001, at the Qala-i-Jangi fortress-prison, a group of foreign prisoners staged a bloody revolt against their guards. The guards, under General Dostum of the Northern Alliance, killed many of the prisoners after the prisoners retrieved weapons from storage trailers and launched a pitched battle. In another case, a group of wounded prisoners in a hospital in Kandahar took over the hospital and fought to the death against Northern Alliance squads sent in to retake the hospital. In some of these cases, the Northern Alliance troops showed no mercy at all to the foreign fighters.

Afghan and international leaders recognized that after the Soviets pulled out in 1989 Afghanistan had been plunged into a civil war. Because they wanted to avoid a similar outcome, the leadership of different factions and parties agreed to try to work out a peaceful interim government to take over after the Taliban left. They held a meeting in Bonn, Germany, in December 2001.

The Bonn meeting brought together prominent Afghans, including many living in exile, together with leaders from the Northern Alliance. To establish a stable government, an Afghan Interim Authority was set up on December 22, 2001. It included 30 members and was to provide a government for six months. That was to be followed by a "Transitional Authority" for two years. The former diplomat and Pashtun leader Hamid Karzai was selected to head the Afghan Interim Authority.

The Bonn Agreement called on the United Nations to set up an International Security Assistance Force (ISAF). The UN acted while the Bonn meeting was still in progress. The UN Security Council passed Resolution 1386 on December 20, 2001. The NATO forces later became part of the UN-authorized ISAF.

The Bonn Agreement also directed the Transitional Authority to convene a national assembly in Afghanistan. In the past, there had been other such assemblies in Afghanistan, known as a *loya jirga*, or grand council. The Bonn Agreement also set up an Afghan Constitution Commission to draft a new constitution for the country.

The new constitution was to be based on the 1964 constitution that had set up reforms in the last years of the monarchy. But before the new peaceful arrangements could be worked out, remaining pockets of Taliban and al-Qaeda presented threats to the plans.

A great many of the al-Qaeda fighters had escaped over the border into Pakistan after the battles at Tora Bora in late 2001. Even so, U.S. intelligence specialists began to look for other places in Afghanistan where both Taliban and al-Qaeda fighters hid out. Early in 2002, U.S. and Northern Alliance forces made a more concerted effort to root out the remaining al-Qaeda strongholds in eastern Afghanistan.

Reports came in that there was a large group of enemy in the Shahi Kowt Valley in the Paktia Province. Many of the people living in this area around Gardez and Khost befriended the Taliban and al-Qaeda. The numbers of Taliban and al-Qaeda fighters there were at first estimated at between 200 and 500. The campaign to get them out, fought over the period March 2 to March 19, 2002, was code-named Operation Anaconda.

A U.S. Army Chinook helicopter off-loads Coalition troops, part of a major operation in 2002 involving U.S., Canadian, and Afghan military forces seeking Osama bin Laden in the Tora Bora Mountains. *(Department of Defense)*

ANACONDA

For Operation Anaconda, the U.S. Special Forces units were orga-nized in Task Force K-Bar, composed of special forces from seven nations, including Norway, New Zealand, Canada, Australia, Germany, and Denmark, as well as the United States. Under the command of Navy SEAL captain Robert Harward, they would work with infantry troops of the Northern Alliance units then working in the Transitional Authority.

The hideout in the Shahi Kowt Valley was in an area about 3 miles wide by six miles long, with three small villages. Most of the valley is itself about 8,000 feet above sea level, with the surrounding mountains reaching up to 11,000 feet. Small trails and goat paths led out through the passes. It was very hard to get firm figures on the number of Taliban and foreign fighters that were in the valley. Estimates ranged from as low as 150 to as high as 1,000.

The original plan had been to use special forces teams with sev-eral hundred Afghan military forces. But as estimates of the enemy numbers increased, the plan expanded to include American troops from the 10th Mountain Division and the 101st Airborne Division. Small special forces units were supplemented by three battalions of U.S. infantry and nearly 1,000 Afghan soldiers who had been trained by U.S. forces.

The operation was carefully planned, with several small forces expected to drive the enemy into fixed positions held by U.S. and Northern Alliance troops. However, when the operation began, advanc-ing trucks soon bogged down in the muddy roads. As the forces moved forward on foot, they began to take fire from enemy mortar and artil-lery concealed in the rocks.

As U.S. forces called in air strikes, they did not hit the intended targets, and the Afghan troops became discouraged. Helicopters bring-ing in more troops were held up by heavy fog in the passes. Attempts to evacuate the wounded resulted in further casualties.

When armored reinforcements, including tanks and personnel carriers, finally came into the valley, the enemy simply fled their positions, leaving behind a few wounded. Canadian and Australian units participated in clearing the valley. When the operation con-cluded, estimates of the enemy killed varied from 100 to as many as 1,000.

It was clear after the battle that most of the enemy had again escaped from the mountain valley through passes. As in the earlier escape, they went into safe hideouts inside Pakistan. Even though an unknown number of enemy got out of the trap, Operation Anaconda turned out to be one of the largest ground battles fought by U.S. and allied forces against the Taliban and al-Qaeda in the whole of the Afghanistan conflict to that time. But its results were meager.

U.S. troops would remain in the country for several years and continue to participate in efforts to track down and eliminate terrorists and Taliban fighters. However, the number of U.S. troops killed in military action in the country remained very low. As the war in Iraq that began in 2003 produced much greater numbers of U.S. casualties, the war in Afghanistan drew far less coverage in the U.S. media, partly because it was far less dangerous for the U.S. troops.

After 2002, the mission of the ISAF evolved and changed. ISAF was limited to about 6,000 troops, and at first they largely worked in policing and training jobs in and around Kabul. The U.S. troops and some of the allied groups operated under the separate U.S. Operation Enduring Freedom until 2006. In 2006, some U.S. troops participated in ISAF, while other U.S. troops still worked under their own command. By 2008, the total number of foreign troops in the country was more than 50,000, including by that time, more than 20,000 U.S. soldiers.

The commitment of international troops under UN auspices became extremely complicated. Each country set up its own rules regarding how its troops could be used. In some cases, the troops were prohibited from engaging in any sort of military exchange with Taliban or al-Qaeda forces. Others had separate rules of engagement. Some countries contributed only a dozen or two dozen troops at a time. But some others provided hundreds or even thousands of troops. Political forces in the home countries sometimes resulted in sudden changes in the number of troops in Afghanistan or changes in how they could be employed.

There were many governmental and nongovernmental organizations (NGOs) working in Afghanistan to improve conditions. But they often appeared to be making little headway. There were as many as 16 different UN agencies at work. Each UN agency had specific goals. These included the Food and Agricultural Organization (FAO), the

CASUALTY RATES

Casualty rates for U.S. troops in Afghanistan remained low, and over the years 2001 to 2008, the number of battle fatalities in the whole country per year remained less than the number of victims of homicide in major U.S. cities such as Philadelphia or Washington, D.C.

Coalition Military Fatalities in Afghanistan by Year

Year	U.S.	Other Allies	Total
2009	316	204	520
2008	155	139	294
2007	117	115	232
2006	98	93	191
2005	99	31	130
2004	52	6	58
2003	48	9	57
2002	49	20	69
2001	12	0	12

The Taliban insurgency increased considerably after 2005, helping to account for the approximate doubling of the casualty rate among U.S. troops from the numbers of 2002 to 2004 to the greater numbers in 2005 and later. Some observers believed that the Taliban also began to intentionally target some of the smaller contingents of non-U.S. troops in order to increase pressure on other countries to withdraw their forces.

World Health Organization (WHO), and the UN Office on Drugs and Crime (UNODC). Some of the others were the World Food Program (WFP), the UN Development Program (UNDP), and the UN Educational, Social, and Cultural Organization (UNESCO).

NGOs and government agency offices went through a cycle that often spent great amounts of money simply in getting established but showing very few positive results in the country. Typically, when a new agency or organization arrived in Afghanistan, it would open an office. It would take over a building and find it needed repairs. Then it would equip it with phones, fax machines, copying machines, and computers. Then it would find it needed a diesel generator because the electric power system was unreliable.

U.S. Navy SEALs, such as these members of one of the U.S. military's most highly trained and versatile Special Operations branches, conducted a variety of specialized operations in Afghanistan. All these men—except Hospital Corpsman 2nd Class Marcus Luttrell *(third from right)*—perished in Operation Red Wing, and group leader Lt. Michael P. Murphy *(end right)* was awarded the Congressional Medal of Honor posthumously. *(U.S. Navy)*

Meanwhile, the staff would need to find housing, which usually had to be repaired. Then the officials would hire a cook, a driver, and other household help. Often those who would be hired would need to speak English, French, or German. So they would usually be men and women educated abroad, like engineers or other professionals. Once the NGO set up offices and housing, they had to hire security guards to prevent the equipment and furniture from being stolen and to protect the staff.

Before the first dollar was spent on helping solve real problems in Afghanistan, the agency or NGO would have spent a large budget on getting set up and hiring people to make their life more comfortable. It took a long time to direct their efforts, money, and education to solving problems. Even so, the number of aid projects around the country continued to grow, gradually bringing schools, clinics, and adult education programs. By 2006, there were an estimated 800 NGOs operating in Afghanistan.

Some projects managed by the military Provincial Reconstruction Teams (PRTs) did other kinds of work. The military units built or repaired roads and bridges. They also built hospitals, housing, water supplies, and markets. Some brought in contractors to get electric power up and running.

Despite the dozens of good projects going on around the country, relief workers, teachers, and health workers faced continuing problems. The many agencies and offices rarely coordinated their work. Fund-

ISAF TROOP COMMITMENTS

Although the figures of troop commitments varied from month to month and even from day to day, the following official figures released in October 2008 gave some indication of the numbers of troops provided by the different countries at that time.

United States	20,600 (total number of U.S. troops in Afghanistan was 32,500 including National Guard)
United Kingdom	8,330
Germany	3,310
France	2,730
Canada	2,500
Italy	2,350
Netherlands	1,770
Poland	1,600
Turkey	1,300
Australia	1,080
Spain	780
Denmark	750
Romania	730
Norway	588
Sweden	500
Bulgaria	460
Belgium	420
Czech Republic	415

ing depended on contributions or budgeted appropriations that varied from year to year and would diminish with economic hard times in the donor countries.

Taliban insurgents and criminals found it easy to target unprotected schools, medical facilities, and other physical structures set up by the relief workers. The raiders could destroy them or loot their equipment for sale. The government had few police to help protect such targets. Furthermore, when a relief or reconstruction effort succeeded, journalists did not usually treat such good news as news. So it was rare that outsiders heard about any progress inside Afghanistan at all.

U.S. Air Force personnel hold the NATO flag at Kandahar airfield during a historic ceremony on July 31, 2007, when the U.S. Air Force turned over command of the airfield to the U.K. Royal Air Force. *(Department of Defense)*

Countries with less than 400 troops each in October 2008 included, among others, Albania, Croatia, Finland, Portugal, and the former Yugoslavia republic of Macedonia.

All of those mentioned above are NATO members except the following: Albania, Australia, Croatia, Finland, Republic of Macedonia, and Sweden.

PROVINCIAL RECONSTRUCTION TEAMS

Many of the foreign troops became engaged in reconstruction projects to help the Afghan people rebuild their devastated country. Provincial Reconstruction Teams (PRTs) were established, with a wide variety of projects under their administration. Since many of the contributing countries did not want their troops to be engaged in military action, many of the international units under ISAF eventually took on reconstruction projects. By 2006 and later, the PRTs were well established, with different national contingents working in different parts of Afghanistan.

American-run PRTs were found in the southern Pashtun provinces.

Spain and Italy ran PRTs in western provinces.

Britain ran PRTs in Mazar-e Sharif and Maimana in the north-central region.

Germany and the Netherlands operated PRTs in the northeastern provinces.

Korea, Lithuania, and New Zealand operated PRTs in central mountainous regions.

Growing out of military aid projects first established by U.S. army units called Joint Reconstruction Teams, the plan was enthusiastically supported by the Interim Afghan Authority in December 2002, and the name was changed to Provincial Reconstruction Teams.

The first PRT established in Afghanistan was in Gardez in January 2003. By June 2005, 20 PRTs were under way, 13 of which were under the leadership of the forces organized in the U.S.-led Operation Enduring Freedom, and seven of which were run by NATO and other

By 2002, it was clear that the regular forces of the Taliban army had been defeated. But the nature of war and peace in Afghanistan made it very difficult to understand exactly what constituted victory in that country. In one sense, it seemed that the war in Afghanistan continued. U.S. soldiers and soldiers from the UN-approved international force continued to be killed and wounded. For such troops, the war had not ended but kept right on going after the defeat of the Taliban and the escape of their leadership to Pakistan.

The country remained in turmoil as armed groups of Taliban continued to attack both the Afghan government and the foreign troops allied nations. The PRTs varied a great deal in scope and number of troops assigned. For example, the British PRT in Mazar-e Sharif had about 100 troops in 2006, while the German PRT in Kunduz had about 375. Most of the PRTs run by the United States had between 60 and 80 staff assigned.

A U.S. Army soldier from a Provincial Reconstruction Team hands out clothing and items for personal hygiene during a humanitarian assistance mission at a women's center near Bagram. *(Department of Defense)*

and aid workers. Some of the Taliban fighters operated in very small groups, coming in from safe havens over the border in Pakistan. Such attacks increased after 2006. Meanwhile, bandits, gangs, and remnants of radical mujahideen contributed to the lawless conditions. Opium dealers operated openly, bribing both local police and high government officials to look the other way.

The Afghan army and police remained poorly trained and extremely unreliable. Some police were corrupt, taking bribes to ignore crimes in their regions. Often, former warlords were appointed as heads of police units and continued to exploit people in their regions.

There was no clearly defined enemy that could be tracked down and defeated. The U.S. mode of warfare, which usually required a defined defeat of the enemy and a conclusive treaty that established the peace, seemed very unsuited to the situation in Afghanistan. The efforts of the Afghan government and the international community to bring peace to the country and the debates about how best to do that are the subjects of the following chapters.

THE ADMINISTRATION OF HAMID KARZAI

The Bonn Agreement in December 2001 set up the civilian government of Afghanistan, at first on an interim or temporary basis. The Interim Government called meetings of the leaders in Afghanistan and held elections. To many outsiders, the system they set up seemed good for the nation.

The Bonn meeting participants made a good effort to include most of Afghanistan's ethnic and political groups. However, the government outlawed the Taliban and its leaders. The government outlawed another political party as well, the faction headed by Gulbuddin Hekmatyar.

Hekmatyar's radical branch of the Islamist Party had received more help from the United States and from Saudi Arabia during the resistance to the Soviets than any other faction. But since then, Hekmatyar had thrown his support to the Taliban. So the new regime outlawed his party as well as the Taliban itself. Hekmatyar would later give more political and military support to the Taliban and al-Qaeda fighters against NATO and U.S. troops.

The Bonn meeting group settled on a moderate leader with a solid background. They needed someone who had support among the Pashtun people to head the temporary government. They chose Hamid Karzai.

Karzai was born on December 24, 1957, in the village of Karz, near the Pashtun city of Kandahar. In Afghanistan, family and clan position are very important for winning support. Karzai's grandfather had served as a deputy Speaker of the senate under the old monarchy. Hamid Karzai's father had been a tribal elder of the Popalzai tribe.

U.S. secretary of defense Donald Rumsfeld, Afghanistan interim authority
chairman Hamid Karzai, and Afghanistan counselor on international relations
Mohammad Marufi meet in April 2002 to discuss security issues facing the
new government. *(Department of Defense)*

Hamid Karzai's father had also served as a deputy Speaker of the parliament in the 1960s.

After Hamid Karzai graduated from high school in 1976, he went
to India to study international relations and political science. While
there, he earned a master's degree at India's Simla University in 1983.
The Soviet army had moved into Afghanistan in 1979. As soon as he
finished his degree, Karzai joined the mujahideen that opposed the
Soviets and the Communist government of Afghanistan, although he
worked as a civilian leader, not as a soldier in that resistance. In 1985,
Karzai took a short course in France in journalism. Then he returned
to work with the resistance to the Soviets. He worked in the moderate Afghanistan National Liberation Front. Sebqhatullah Mojadeddi
led that party, and Karzai served as the director of information. That
meant that he handled relations with the news media.

After the Soviets left the country, some of the mujahideen factions
formed a government in exile in Pakistan. Mojadeddi headed that
government from 1989 to 1992. When the government took over in
Kabul in 1992, Mojadeddi appointed Karzai as deputy foreign minister.
Karzai served in that post between 1992 and 1996.

After the Taliban took power in Afghanistan in 1996, they began to kill leaders of the former government, including some members of Karzai's own family. He went into exile in Quetta, a city just over the border inside Pakistan. He returned to Afghanistan in October 2001 and led the resistance to the Taliban around Kandahar in the last days of the Taliban regime. On December 5, 2001, the participants in the Bonn meeting chose Karzai to head the new Interim Administration.

Karzai seemed an ideal candidate. He could speak English and French. He had experience in journalism and foreign policy. His reputation as a moderate looked good. Afghans also found it important that he came from a well-connected family of Pashtun people.

LOYA JIRGA

In Afghanistan, it has been a long tradition to call a grand national council from time to time. They are used to obtain a national agreement or consensus on major political issues. A wide variety of clan leaders, local dignitaries, and village elders attend these meetings. The leaders in these assemblies are usually well-known local leaders, not formally elected but accepted as representative of their clans, villages, and neighborhoods.

Such a grand national assembly or council is known as a *loya jirga*. In the past, such assemblies were only attended by Pashtun people. They were sometimes called to install a new king. For instance, a *loya jirga* was called in 1930 to confirm the installation of Nadir Shah as king.

King Nadir Shah called other *loya jirgas* in 1941, 1949, and 1964. The 1941 meeting declared Afghanistan neutral in World War II. The 1949 *loya jirga* disapproved the Durand Line as a border with Pakistan. The 1964 *loya jirga* approved a constitution for the monarchy.

A *loya jirga* in 1985 replaced the monarchy with the republic of Afghanistan. The Bonn meeting in December 2001 was not a full *loya jirga,* but it reflected the same idea of a grand council. A formal meeting of a *loya jirga* met on June 13, 2002, to appoint Hamid Karzai as president of the Afghan Transitional Administration. This meeting had about 2,000 people in attendance and met in a tent on the grounds of Kabul Polytechnic School. Another was held in December 2003. That meeting ratified the new constitution of the country.

The choice of Hamid Karzai, a Pashtun, helped make the new government seem less like one put in place by the minority Tajiks and Uzbeks of the Northern Alliance. He appointed a cabinet made up of a variety of people. Some had been military officers. Others had been professors and specialists in technical fields. Some had been living abroad. He included prominent members of the different political parties and different ethnic groups. He and his cabinet took office on December 22, 2001.

The interim government only lasted about six months under the plan. The interim government convened a *loya jirga,* on June 13, 2002. That meeting set up a transitional government and elected Hamid Karzai as president. Two years later, on October 9, 2004, he won a majority of votes in a well-conducted national presidential election.

In that election, more than 8 million Afghans voted. Women made up about 41 percent of the voters. Election monitors announced Karzai as the winner on November 2, 2004. He won a five-year term, to expire in May 2009. Due to the unsettled state of the country, his term was

An Afghan voter displays his finger, stained to show he has voted in the first post-liberation parliamentary elections in Afghanistan on September 18, 2005. *(Department of Defense)*

later extended to October 2009. He formally took office as president on December 7, 2004. Diplomats and world leaders came to Afghanistan for the inauguration. They hoped the ceremony represented the step to democracy and peace that the country needed and hoped for.

With his moderate political background and his reputation for concern for human rights, outsiders thought that he would be a good uniting force for the country. He had been an advocate of improving the status of women and protecting all human rights. He appointed three women to his first cabinet. He later appointed a woman as a provincial governor.

Afghanistan held another election on September 18, 2005, for the Wolesi Jirga, or lower house, of the new two-chambered National Assembly. The election also chose members for each of the 34 provincial councils. In this election, fewer voters turned out, about 53 percent of the 12.5 million voters who had been registered. An indirect method chose the members of the upper house, or Meshrano Jirga. The provincial councils selected two-thirds of the members, and the president appointed the other one-third.

After the 2005 elections, the first complete and properly chosen National Assembly in Afghanistan since the 1960s took office on December 19, 2005. Sebqhatullah Mojadeddi, the leader of the moderate party, won election as head of the upper house of the assembly.

During the elections, a voter would get his or her finger dyed with a purple dye to stop people voting more than once. Pictures of proud Afghans holding up their dyed fingers showed proof they had voted in a free election. Those pictures inspired hope around the world that Afghanistan might have a democratic government.

However, the war in Afghanistan kept up, although at a low level. The fighting led to a small and increasing stream of casualties to the U.S. and other foreign troops in the country. Hamid Karzai faced many problems. Political parties disagreed over policy. The history of the country worked against a powerful central government. Afghans disagreed over Islamic culture. Even the fight against crime made problems for Hamid Karzai.

Hamid Karzai and his government faced many problems familiar to those who have studied the history of Afghanistan. The democratically elected regime of Karzai faced the hostility of local leaders and warlords. The same problem had faced the monarchy and the Communist government. Afghans of all ethnic groups preferred to have

POLITICAL PARTIES IN AFGHANISTAN

Under the Afghan constitution, it is fairly easy to organize a new political party. To register as a legal party, the group has to have at least 700 members signed up. It has to promise *not* to have a military component. It also has to promise to restrict its activities to political affairs, such as publishing a newspaper and running candidates for public office.

Under these rules, many of the older mujahideen parties registered. Other new factions and new groups also registered as parties. By 2005, there were at least 65 registered political parties, many of them quite small. The list of 65 legal parties did not include any that were based in foreign countries.

Hamid Karzai was himself an independent without a political party affiliation. However, Karzai had previously served in the cabinet headed by Burhanuddin Rabbani, the leader of the Islamic Society of Afghanistan.

Some of the largest parties were:

Afghan Mellat or **Afghan Social Democratic Party.** This is the largest Pashtun nationalist party. Some members of this party serve in Hamid Karzai's cabinet.

Islamic Society of Afghanistan. This party was led by Burhanuddin Rabbani, who had been a leader of the country in the early 1990s. Karzai has appointed several leaders of this party to important positions.

Islamic Unity Party of the People of Afghanistan. This party is very powerful among the Hazara people. Some of Karzai's strongest opponents are organized in this party.

National Congress Party of Afghanistan. This party ran a campaign for Abdul Latif Pedram as a candidate for president against Karzai in 2004 and lost.

National Islamic Movement of Afghanistan. This party is led by the former mujahideen general Dostum, an Uzbek. He had been prominent in the Northern Alliance.

New Afghanistan Party. This group has tried to form an alliance between many smaller parties.

local and trusted families in charge. They wanted them to run the police, roads, and courts. They did not want appointees from a distant government in Kabul.

Even when the central authority picked out local leaders, other families and clans in provinces would claim that they could be better at representing local interests. Although Karzai came from a well-known family and clan of Pashtun ethnicity, many workers in his government departments came from the former Northern Alliance groups of Uzbek and Tajiks. Pashtuns saw them as foreigners when they came to their villages.

Traditionally, a commitment to drive out foreigners from power in Afghanistan tended to unite Afghans across political, ethnic, and religious lines. The more that NATO and American forces and foreign NGOs worked in the country, the more resentment against them increased. Everything the central government did to impose order and rebuild the country could seem bad to local leaders. They viewed such work as either interference from the distant Kabul central government or the work of foreigners, or both. So Karzai's appointed leaders and the foreign troops naturally became targets of traditional resentment.

These traditional factors made it very difficult for Hamid Karzai. The more he cooperated with the American and ISAF forces, the more he could be seen as a foreign puppet. On the other hand, the more he disagreed or refused to cooperate with the Americans and the other foreign forces, the more he would offend them and weaken their support of him.

Some special problems came up with the people that Karzai appointed. Karzai put the former military commander Abdul Karim Khoram in charge of cultural and youth affairs. However, Khoram used his position to try to suppress the use of the Dari language. Dari is similar to the Farsi language used in Iran. When some students put up a sign in Dari that meant "University" rather than the Pashtun sign, he had them arrested. Furthermore, he began to impose strict limits on what sorts of television shows could be broadcast, clamping down on the showing of Indian-made movies. Some of those movies would show men and women dancing together, which he felt violated good standards of behavior. The station Tolo TV had broadcast the films. The managers of that station protested the action. Khoram told them that they had to stop broadcasting such material because it offended Islamic standards of morality.

Others besides Khoram joined in the attack on television content. The Wolesi Jirga, the lower house of parliament, adopted a resolution in 2008 ordering all Afghan media to stop carrying images they called "sensual." The congregation of Muslim clergy known as the Council of Ulemas joined in. They also asked President Karzai to ban Tolo TV and other TV stations because of what they regarded as anti-Islamic programming.

A few members of parliament regarded these actions as violations of freedom of the press. But some of the conservative members of parliament wanted the government to close down the offending TV stations. These sorts of conflicts showed the difficulties of operat-

AFGHANISTAN CABINET MEMBERS

Hamid Karzai appointed men and women with a wide variety of backgrounds to serve in his first cabinet. A large number of them were people who had to go into exile during the Communist rule or the Taliban government. Some of these were educated abroad in England, Germany, or the United States. Some of them received higher degrees in international relations, development, administration, and other fields. Some had taught in universities abroad or in Afghanistan. Such people are often called technocrats because they are less interested in politics and are technical specialists in the fields in which they work.

In countries suffering from political turmoil such as Afghanistan, technocrats are often chosen to fill important government positions. Leaders believe that technocrats might focus their energies on getting things running smoothly. Usually they do not get too interested in running for office. Since they usually do not have the backing of a political party or faction, it is easy for the president to fire them or move them from job to job. However, the drawback is that they do not have a political party to support them in their work and their decisions.

A few of the cabinet officers were military or political leaders of the mujahideen, and some of them represented several of the many political parties of Afghanistan. Karzai has tried to appoint leaders from different ethnic groups and leaders from both the Sunni and Shia branches of Islam. However, Abdul Karim Khoram (in charge of cultural and youth affairs), is strongly anti-Shia, as well as being committed to a strict view of Islamic morality.

ing a democracy when many of the elected members did not believe in freedom of choice about television shows and other forms of free speech.

Because of the many difficulties of governing all of Afghanistan from the capital, some journalists took up calling Karzai "the mayor of Kabul," suggesting that his power really did not go beyond the capital. Others charged him and members of his family and cabinet with corruption, taking bribes or kickbacks in money.

Other problems abounded. By 2008, 93 percent of the world's heroin supply came from the opium poppies grown in Afghanistan. Whole regions of the country that had been devastated by war had

Karzai is the first president of Afghanistan to appoint women to the cabinet. In the year 2003, he appointed Mrs. Husn Banu Ghazanfar as minister of women's affairs. She taught at Kabul University and then studied in St. Petersburg, Russia. She returned to serve as chairperson of the literature department at Kabul University.

President Karzai eventually moved several cabinet members from one position to another. In at least one case, he fired a cabinet member for corruption. Most of the cabinet members spoke several languages.

Karzai's choices for cabinet members represented an effort to satisfy different political constituencies, while for the most part selecting technocrats rather than rival prominent politicians. Whether these choices were best for the country has remained controversial.

Joining generals from the Afghan and U.S. armies in cutting a cake at the International Women's Day celebration at Bagram Air Base on March 3, 2008, was Mrs. Husn Banu Ghazanfar *(center)*, the minister of women's affairs, the only woman in President Karzai's cabinet at that time. Such an office, and its inclusion on such an occasion, would have been unheard of under the Taliban government. *(Department of Defense)*

Afghan National Army soldiers display more than six kilos of opium discovered in a former insurgent safe house in Afghanistan. Afghanistan is the world's largest grower of opium, and it is known that the sale of opium is probably the major source of income for the Taliban. *(Department of Defense)*

given up other forms of traditional agriculture. Instead, they relied on raising and selling opium.

Most of the money from opium went to gangsters, smugglers, and dope dealers outside of Afghanistan. Even so, the farmers' revenue from opium made it seem like the best crop. When U.S. forces tried to suppress the opium growing by destroying the crops in the field, they only made the local people resent U.S. forces even more.

Afghanistan's own army and police did not take up the job of policing the country. Few qualified people wanted to volunteer for those dangerous jobs. Sometimes when a new police recruit got his weapons, he would be mugged in the street a few days later and his weapons taken away. Reports came out that other policemen beat up the recruits, stole their weapons, and then sold the weapons on the black market. Such weapons would then be bought by Taliban or gangsters.

When foreign police experts tried to come in to teach classes in police procedure, they would find it almost impossible to teach the young recruits. Many of them had never been in a classroom of any kind before and did not understand that they had to listen and learn. When instructors would bring up a subject like protection of women's rights, the young recruits would burst out laughing. They thought the idea that women had rights was a joke.

All of these problems made it extremely difficult for the administration of Hamid Karzai to bring order to the country. Karzai had to face the traditional distrust of foreign support. He had to deal with crime and corruption. He could not control the countryside.

In the United States, Americans worried about the troops bogged down in the war in Iraq that went on from 2003 to 2010. The terrible news and worse casualty figures from Iraq often pushed the news about Afghanistan off the front pages. Even so, Americans debated the war in Afghanistan as well as the war in Iraq during the same period. The next chapter discusses those debates and disagreements.

U.S. DEBATES
OVER POLICY

As a free people, Americans have always debated about whether or not their wars were justified and whether they were being fought properly. In the case of the war in Afghanistan, the debates that began 2001 were made more complicated by the fact that the United States soon got involved in another war. That other war, in Iraq, began in March 2003.

The United States and Coalition partners, including Britain, launched an attack on the regime of Saddam Hussein in Iraq in March 2003. Within two months, the Iraqi army was defeated and the leaders of Hussein's regime were either captured or had gone into hiding.

In May 2003, President George W. Bush, in a public appearance that returned to haunt him, spoke before a banner on a U.S. Navy aircraft carrier that read "Mission Accomplished." Unfortunately, as Americans were to learn over the next six years, it would cost more than 4,000 American lives before the United States could even plan for the withdrawal.

The details of the Iraq War and its extended aftermath are covered in another volume in this series. Yet since that war continued while the war in Afghanistan went on, events in Iraq affected events in Afghanistan.

As news of casualties continued to flow from Iraq, Americans wondered why the defeat of the large Iraqi army and the apparent military victory had not brought peace. Although there was no clearly defined enemy after May 2003, the war in Iraq dragged on.

There was no Taliban in Iraq, but members of Hussein's Baath Party and former officers of his army participated in resistance. They were joined by others, including militant leaders of the Shia majority. These latter had resented the dominance of Hussein with his largely Sunni leadership. Many Sunni leaders also resisted the American occupation.

David Petraeus, commanding general of the Multi-National Force — Iraq,
President George W. Bush, and Admiral William J. Fallon, commander of
the U.S. Central Command, conducted a surprise visit with Iraqi government
officials in September 2007. *(Department of Defense)*

Although the resistance to the American occupation and to the new
central government of Iraq was diverse in its makeup, the U.S. press
tended to call all the armed resistance groups "insurgents."

Members of al-Qaeda worked with this resistance and fueled
hatreds between Sunnis and Shias. Only in the northern region, largely
populated by Kurds, was there any peace and reconstruction. Former
Baathists, foreign jihadists, al-Qaeda leaders, and militant religious
factions kept Iraq in turmoil.

U.S. troops faced many threats. There were suicide bombers and improvised explosive devices (IEDs). Patrols met sniper attacks. U.S. Army and Marines fought major pitched battles and uprisings in the so-called Sunni Triangle to the north and west of Baghdad, the capital city. Even though there was no declared war against a clear national government, the level of U.S. casualties meant that hostilities continued.

Americans debated whether the Iraq War was justified. That sometimes bitter debate overshadowed the war in Afghanistan in the public eye. Television and newspapers might mention an occasional event in Afghanistan. But the focus of newswriters, television anchors, and politicians remained on Iraq.

The United States had fought wars on more than one front or area of operations in the past, as in World War II. In that war there had been a European theater and a Pacific theater. The U.S. Army and Air Force focused mostly on Europe, while the U.S. Navy and Marines fought many battles in the Pacific. Americans kept up with the news from both theaters.

However, the two wars in the first decade of the 21st century had few similarities. The need to bring peace to the countryside and the need to develop counterinsurgency methods were similar. But the details on the ground were very different.

To many Americans, it seemed that the war in Iraq had no clear justification. The U.S. administration and UN observers had been quite convinced that Saddam Hussein was developing weapons of mass destruction (WMD). That term includes poison gas, biological weapons, and nuclear weapons. However, when Iraq was defeated, U.S. troops found only small stockpiles of older poison gas weapons and no evidence that nuclear or biological weapons programs had ever existed.

As the number of U.S. casualties in Iraq continued to rise in the face of resistance, many U.S. political leaders who had voted to approve of the war and its funding believed that they had been deceived. Many in the American public felt the same way. Critics believed that the war in Iraq was unjustified. They also believed that American lives were being wasted there for no good purpose. As a consequence, public support for the war in Iraq declined from a clear majority in 2003 to a clear minority by 2006.

This change in public opinion had repercussions for how Americans treated the war in Afghanistan. One development was that the

CONTRASTS AND SIMILARITIES

Although Afghanistan is a much larger country than Iraq (250,000 square miles compared to 168,000 square miles), Iraq's population is much larger—more than 60 million to Afghanistan's 15 million. The Bush administration hoped to establish a workable democracy in Iraq that would set an example for the rest of the region. Because Iraq borders on Iran and Syria, two countries that have supported terrorism, it seemed possible that a major democracy in their midst might help bring pressure on them to reform.

Iraq was far more modern and developed than Afghanistan, and it had large oil resources. If those resources could be restored and developed, the country would have economic resources to continue modernization.

In contrast to Iraq, Afghanistan is one of the poorest countries in the world. While Iraq could make millions from oil exports, Afghanistan has no major export product, except an illegal one, opium.

Iraq is divided by ethnicity and religion into three regions: In the north are the Kurds; concentrated in the center are the Sunni; and concentrated in the south are the Shia. The less traditional Sunni are fewer in number than the Shia, but under Saddam Hussein they came to totally dominate the government and economy. Although the three groups remain hostile to each other, the country has a stronger tradition of a powerful central government than does Afghanistan.

Iraq, like Afghanistan, has long borders that are hard to patrol or protect. Support and weapons for terrorists can come into Iraq from Syria and Iran. In Afghanistan, most of the outside support for terrorists came from the remote regions of Pakistan.

Both countries have conflicts between Sunni and Shia. In Iraq, the Shia suffered discrimination under the regime of Saddam Hussein. In Afghanistan, the Shia are a minority and tend to be despised and held down by the Sunni.

Most Iraqis speak Arabic, although in the northern region the dominant language is Kurdish. In Afghanistan, the largest language group consists of Pashtuns who speak an Indo-European language. However, they make up only about 40 percent of the population. The rest speak a variety of other languages.

heated debates and news about Iraq continued to push the news of Afghanistan off the front pages and make the latter seem "the forgotten war." Another result was that in the debates over Iraq, many political leaders took the position that the war in Iraq was "the bad war" and that "the good war" in Afghanistan had been neglected. They believed it was neglected, not only in the press, but in resources and effort.

The major reason for the good war/bad war distinction had to do with the causes of the wars. Most Americans continued to believe that it was the right thing to do to try to track down Osama bin Laden and the other leaders of al-Qaeda. They were the criminals who had planned and financed the 9/11 attacks. The fact that the oppressive Afghan government of the Taliban had protected bin Laden seemed to offer a double justification for the war in Afghanistan. They had not only harbored a major criminal organization, but they had suppressed human rights horribly.

The Iraq situation was different. There was no evidence that Saddam Hussein and his government had any knowledge of the 9/11 attacks before they happened. Even though many Americans believed his government supported terrorism, there was no clear link between that regime and the 9/11 attacks on America. When it turned out that there were no active nuclear weapons in Iraq, many Americans believed that the war there had no justification at all. Many blamed Bush and his advisers such as Vice President Dick Cheney and Defense Secretary Donald Rumsfeld for getting the United States into a war that lacked broad international support.

President Bush continued to view the two wars as part of the same war on terror. In his annual State of the Union speech given in January 2004, he made it clear that he viewed the war in Afghanistan as an important part of that effort. He pointed to progress in Afghanistan:

> The first to see our determination were the Taliban, who made Afghanistan the training base of al-Qaeda killers. As of this month, that country has a new constitution, guaranteeing free elections and full participation by women. Businesses are opening, health care centers are being established, and the boys and girls of Afghanistan are back in school. . . . The men and women of Afghanistan are building a nation that is free, and proud, and fighting terror—and America is honored to be their friend.

At that time, the war in Afghanistan seemed to be going well. It was also true that the number of U.S. troops committed to Afghanistan was much lower than the number in Iraq.

President Bush and his advisers continued to argue that fighting against insurgents in Iraq showed the American commitment to oppose terrorism and to support democracy. More and more, however, journalists and political leaders criticized that view, believing that the U.S. military effort to bring stability to Iraq only fed the arguments of those who hated the United States in the Middle East region.

Critics against the war in Iraq further argued that President Bush had lost the support of the world community, even though a number of other countries continued to participate in the forces in Iraq. The war in Iraq became one of the major issues in the 2004 presidential election in the United States.

In 2004, Senator John F. Kerry was chosen as the Democratic Party nominee for the presidency. He made it part of his campaign to criticize President Bush for placing more emphasis on the war in Iraq than on the war in Afghanistan. Like many others, Senator Kerry had originally supported both wars. But as time went on, he concluded that the war in Afghanistan was more justified and appropriate than the war in Iraq.

By 2007, the opposition to the war in Iraq had grown very strong. President Bush's popularity severely declined because of it. Despite advice from many military advisers, he supported a plan to increase the troop levels in Iraq. This policy became known as the surge of troops.

President Bush announced the policy on January 10, 2007. He called it a new way forward. Opponents remained highly critical, viewing it as a form of escalation. That word recalled the policy of Lyndon Johnson, who in the 1960s continued to send greater numbers of troops to Vietnam. Escalation had not worked, they argued. The surge would not work either. But Bush sent another 30,000 U.S. troops to Iraq.

Whether it was entirely due to this surge of troops or to a combination of factors, the rate of American casualties was declining by 2009, and there were some signs of increased political stability in the country. Within a year, polls of American public opinion showed that larger numbers of the American people believed that the war in Iraq was going better than it had before. Opponents were still angry over the presence of U.S. troops in Iraq, but even they had to admit that it seemed that the surge of troop strength had some good results.

JOHN KERRY ON AFGHANISTAN

During the presidential election of 2004, the Democratic Party nominated Senator John F. Kerry for the presidency. During the presidential election campaign, there were three televised debates. John Kerry made it part of his campaign to directly accuse President Bush of having misdirected attention from Afghanistan to conduct the war in Iraq. In the first debate, Senator Kerry said:

> The president just talked about Iraq as a center of the war on terror. Iraq was not even close to the center of the war on terror before the president invaded it. The president made the judgment to divert forces from under General Tommy Franks from Afghanistan before the Congress even approved it to begin to prepare to go to war in Iraq. And he rushed the war in Iraq without a plan to win the peace. Now, that is not the judgment that a president of the United States ought to make. You don't take America to war unless [you] have the plan to win the peace. . . . Saddam Hussein didn't attack us. Osama bin Laden attacked us. Al-Qaeda attacked us. And when we had Osama bin Laden cornered in the mountains of Tora Bora, he had 1,000 of his cohorts with him in those mountains. With the American military forces nearby and in the field, we didn't use the best trained troops in the world to go kill the world's number one criminal and terrorist.

Senator Kerry also claimed that by having members of the Northern Alliance attempt to track down Osama bin Laden, President Bush had outsourced the war. The Bush administration claimed that they had relied on Afghan forces because they did not want it to appear that the United States was trying to control Afghanistan.

In 2008, the two major nominees for the U.S. presidency were both senators. John McCain, a Republican, had a reputation for independence. Democratic senator Barack Obama was the first African American to run for the presidency on a major party ticket. Senator Obama indicated that if he were elected he would plan on a reduction of troop strength in Iraq. He committed to a withdrawal of all combat troops in that country within 16 or 18 months of being inaugurated. Senator McCain did not believe that setting a specific time frame for

Even though he was defeated for the presidency in 2004, Senator Kerry continued to advocate sending more troops to Afghanistan. Many have seen his arguments contributing to the idea that the war in Afghanistan was a "good war" and that the war in Iraq was a "bad war."

Chairman of the Joint Chiefs of Staff Admiral Mike Mullen and Senator John F. Kerry talk at the U.S. Capitol before the start of the presidential inauguration on January 20, 2009. Senator Kerry would take over as chairman of the Senate Foreign Relations Committee and thus play a crucial role in the future conduct of the war in Afghanistan. *(Department of Defense)*

withdrawal was a good idea, as it might encourage the insurgent groups in Iraq.

Senator Obama also indicated that if he were elected, he would increase the focus on the war in Afghanistan. He echoed the sentiment voiced by Senator Kerry in 2004, that the war in Afghanistan had more justification than the war in Iraq. At the same time, Obama stated that a policy of a surge in troop strength in Afghanistan might increase the chances of establishing peace there.

LAW ENFORCEMENT OR WAR

One of the issues that made the war in Afghanistan controversial was the fact that it had started because the United States had evidence that Osama bin Laden and other leaders of al-Qaeda like Ayman al-Zawahiri had arranged and funded the 9/11 attacks. They had taken up living in Afghanistan when the attacks were launched.

Although the crime was a huge one, the government of Afghanistan had not sanctioned it or been involved in planning it. The emir of Afghanistan and the leader of the Taliban, Mullah Omar, had warned bin Laden against attacking the United States. In Iraq, Saddam Hussein was as surprised as the rest of the world at the events of 9/11.

While Americans were justifiably horrified and angry at the attacks of 9/11, they had not been acts of war by any government.

War as an instrument of policy can best be used against governments. In the heat of anger over 9/11, President George W. Bush as well as Democratic leaders like Hillary Clinton and John Kerry supported the use of military force against the planners of 9/11, even though they were criminals, not the government of a nation.

Many analysts and commentators have pointed out that it is difficult to have a war on terror. Terror is not a place, or a nation, or a government but a method or strategy. In this case, it was a method employed by an international organization of fanatics.

Even so, the defenders of military action have argued that military force was the only way to try to get at bin Laden and his organization. Even Bush's opponents have agreed that since the Taliban government would not cooperate in shutting down bin Laden's camps or in arresting him, the U.S. government was justified in attacking that government.

As the election of 2008 neared, the nation and the world began to face a severe economic crisis. Several large investment companies and banks faced bankruptcy, and unemployment began to increase. Both candidates found themselves more involved in discussing economic conditions than foreign policy. Barack Obama won the presidency with more than 53 percent of the popular vote. Observers expected that as president, he would carry through on the plan to reduce the emphasis on the war in Iraq and to increase the U.S. military presence in Afghanistan. After he was inaugurated, that is exactly what he did.

PAKISTAN AND AFGHANISTAN

When U.S. and Northern Alliance troops tried to arrest the al-Qaeda leaders and the Taliban officials who had protected them in 2001, most of them escaped capture. Many of them fled over the rugged mountain border into neighboring Pakistan, to the east of Afghanistan.

Hiding out in Pakistan was made easier because of several facts. The region, like eastern Afghanistan, is mountainous, with many small villages in high valleys. The larger cities, like Peshawar and Quetta, already housed tens of thousands of refugees from Afghanistan.

Although there were Pakistani government offices in the regions of Pakistan near the border, Baluchistan and North-West Frontier Province, Pakistan did not station any of its army in the region. In North-West Frontier Province, some of the small states and territories were tribally administered, running their own affairs like independent countries. Some were known as tribal agencies.

Furthermore, many of the people in North-West Frontier Province and Baluchistan are Pashtun, the same ethnic group that dominates in southern and eastern Afghanistan. Most of the Taliban were also Pashtun. So it was easy for them to blend into the local population or hide among the Afghan refugees.

The Pashtun people in Pakistan practiced the protection of guests, even when the guests were lawbreakers. For all of these reasons, Pakistan provided a safe haven for the Taliban and al-Qaeda fighters from Afghanistan.

As forces from the United States, NATO, and other countries tried to maintain order in Afghanistan, they realized that Taliban and al-Qaeda fighters coming in from Pakistan represented a threat. So the United States asked the Pakistani government to assist in

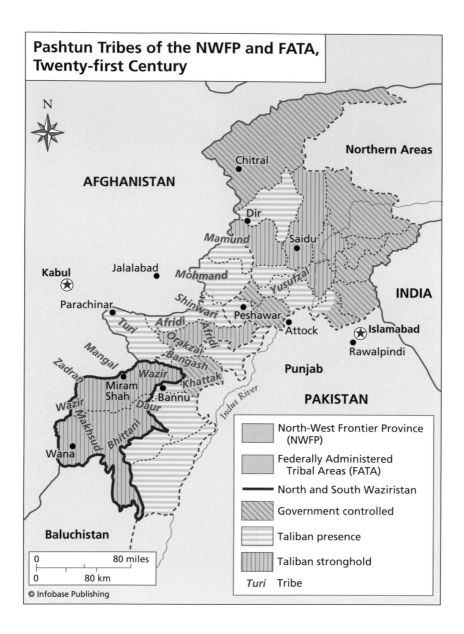

Pashtun Tribes of the NWFP and FATA, Twenty-first Century

Map legend:
- North-West Frontier Province (NWFP)
- Federally Administered Tribal Areas (FATA)
- North and South Waziristan
- Government controlled
- Taliban presence
- Taliban stronghold
- *Turi* Tribe

0   80 miles
0   80 km

© Infobase Publishing

arresting the Taliban and al-Qaeda leaders. When the Pakistanis said that they could not find them, U.S. military authorities grew frustrated.

Furthermore, if the Pakistani authorities openly cooperated with the Americans and NATO troops, it would anger the Pakistani public. They would see such cooperation as giving up Pakistan's independence to foreigners.

PAKISTAN'S HISTORY

In the 19th century, the entire area of what are now Pakistan, India, and Bangladesh was known as the Indian subcontinent. After the failure of a rebellion (the Sepoy mutiny) against the British in 1857, the opposition to British rule took the form of nonviolent political organization and protest. For the most part, that movement was led by people of the Hindu religion. However, a large part of the population of the Indian subcontinent was Muslim.

Muslim leaders began organizing their own movement for independence in the 1930s, known as the All-India Muslim League. When in 1947, Britain granted independence for the whole subcontinent and removed its troops, the area was partitioned into a largely Muslim country, Pakistan, and a largely Hindu country, India.

Benazir Bhutto returned to Pakistan in fall 2007 and appeared on her way to be reelected prime minister in January 2008 when she was assassinated on December 27, 2007. Al-Qaeda immediately took responsibility for the assassination, and it was generally agreed that the assassin belonged to a Pakistani terrorist group that had ties to al-Qaeda. *(Department of Defense)*

Pakistan at that time consisted of two parts, East Pakistan and West Pakistan, with the country of India between them. However, in 1971 East Pakistan, resenting the domination of the region by Punjabis from the West, declared its independence and became the independent country of Bangladesh.

West Pakistan continued to use the name of Pakistan. It consisted of four provinces: West Punjab and Sindh on the eastern side, bordering India, and Baluchistan and North-West Frontier Territories (later known as North-West Frontier Province) on the western side bordering Afghanistan.

India and Pakistan fought three short wars. The first, in 1948, was over the disputed province of Kashmir, and Pakistan continued to occupy a small

(continues)

(continued)

section of that province. The second was in 1971, when India helped East Pakistan secede as Bangladesh. A third short war, the Kargil Conflict, was fought in 1999 in Kashmir over control of that province.

When the Soviet Union provided aid to India, Pakistan sought help from the United States. America provided weapons and aircraft for Pakistan's defense. More than 90 percent of Pakistanis are Muslims, but most are not radical and want to maintain friendship with the United States to help protect them against India. The continuing dispute with India over Kashmir, Pakistani anger over the treatment of Muslims still living in India, and other issues keep Pakistan-India tensions high.

The United States did not want to start a war with Pakistan by invading that country. Pakistan had been an ally of the United States for years. The United States had bases in Pakistan. Americans used Pakistan as a supply route to bring in supplies for the forces in Afghanistan. Other facts about Pakistani history helped explain why the Pakistani border problem was so serious.

Most American leaders believed that it was important to maintain good relations with Pakistan. They wanted to avoid any chance of a war against that country. As an American ally, Pakistan had helped the United States supply weapons to the mujahideen to throw the Soviet troops out of Afghanistan in the 1980s. Pakistan had often provided troops and other help to keep peace around the world. Pakistani soldiers had fought alongside U.S. troops as allies in the Gulf War in 1991. They had served in Bosnia and Somalia as UN peacekeepers in the period of 1992 to 1996.

Another reason that the United States wanted to avoid war with Pakistan was the fact that Pakistan had developed nuclear weapons. Because Pakistan had atomic bombs, any war against Pakistan ran the risk of the use of those weapons. Atomic bombs had not been used in warfare since 1945, when the United States dropped two of them on Japan, ending World War II. The destruction from the weapons was so horrible that no U.S. policy maker wanted to run the risk that another war might involve them.

When the British ruled over the countries that are now Pakistan and India in the period from the 1850s through the 1940s, they worked out boundaries with neighboring countries. The boundary between Baluchistan (now one of the four provinces of Pakistan) and Afghanistan was called the Durand Line. It was named after the British foreign secretary for India Mortimer Durand, who established the line in 1893. The agreement between the British and the Afghanistan government was set for 100 years.

After Pakistan got its independence, it recognized the same boundary. But Afghanistan refused to accept it. In 1993, the Afghan government announced that it would not extend the 100-year-old agreement. They claimed that the boundary had been unfairly set up.

Meanwhile, Pakistan continued to insist that the old colonial boundary was the modern boundary. The reason that Afghanistan did not renew its acceptance of the Durand Line is that many Pashtun live on both sides of the line. Some Afghan leaders could win support

PAKISTAN'S NUCLEAR WEAPONS

Pakistan's nuclear weapons work began in January 1972. It was set up by Zulfikar Ali Bhutto when he was minister for fuel, power and natural resources. Later he became president and prime minister of Pakistan.

In 1974, India tested a nuclear device in an underground test. That made the Pakistanis put more money and work behind their own project. In 1975, Dr. Abdul Qadeer Khan arrived to take over the project. He had received his training in Germany and had worked at a nuclear facility in the Netherlands. Dr. Khan took over the building and operation of the nuclear plant in Kahuta, Pakistan, set up in 1976. At the same time, he began to import restricted technology, materials, and know-how, some of it in violation of international agreements.

By 1986, reports leaked out of Pakistan that it had gathered enough material to build an atomic bomb. However, it was not until 1998 that Pakistan conducted five tests of underground nuclear explosions. The tests were done at a remote site named Ras Koh in Baluchistan Province.

Outside observers, checking seismic and other remote-sensing data, were not sure whether Pakistan had conducted six explosion tests, as they claimed, or whether the total was only three or four. In any case, it was clear that by 1998 Pakistan had developed the ability to conduct a nuclear test, which meant that it probably had nuclear weapons that could be dropped from aircraft.

Secretary of Defense Donald Rumsfeld escorts Pervez Musharraf, president of Pakistan, through an honor cordon during a visit to the Pentagon in February 2002. Although the U.S. government recognized that Musharraf was a virtual dictator, he was regarded as necessary to keep Pakistan's support for U.S. operations in Afghanistan. *(Department of Defense)*

among Afghan Pashtun by suggesting that someday a greater Pashtunistan might be created.

If it were ever set up, Pashtunistan would include territory where Pashtun people lived on the Pakistani side of the Durand Line. Afghanistan has been too weak and divided since 1993 to be able to do much about this claim. But the Pashtunistan idea has given the Pakistani government one more reason not to want Afghanistan to develop a strong and stable government.

The U.S. government complained to Pakistan about the Taliban and al-Qaeda forces in Baluchistan and North-West Frontier Province. So the Pakistani government sent their own army troops into North-West Frontier Province. By the year 2006, the Pakistanis had lost about 700 soldiers in the battles against the local Taliban there. No Pakistani army had ever before been stationed in the two small tribal agencies, North and South Waziristan.

Local leaders hated seeing the Pakistani army come in. Many of them sided with the Taliban. Soon, news came out that the local Taliban leader, Baitullah Mehsud, had a personal army numbering in the tens of thousands in South Waziristan. Rival leaders in the region had similar militias or armies. Like the Pashtun in Afghanistan, the Pakistani Pashtun were used to local commanders or warlords controlling small pockets of territory.

By 2007, the Pakistani government hoped to win over local leaders in the region by making agreements granting even more local control. In exchange, the local militias promised that they would stop the raids by Taliban and al-Qaeda into Afghanistan. They also said they would agree to a truce in the battles against the Pakistani army.

In several small territories, including Bajaur, North and South Waziristan, and Swat, the Pakistani government agreed to let the local people close down the law courts. They let the local people begin ruling on cases through the religious courts, imposing their own version of sharia.

Swat is a province high in the mountains with beautiful valleys. Some tourists compared it to Switzerland for its beauty and climate. The local party leaders who took control over Swat called themselves the Taliban. They were a local version of the Taliban, separate from the Afghan Taliban. However, it was a fact that the Pakistani government had turned over control of a local region to a Taliban group. Many in the United States and Europe worried that this change would mean more trouble, not less trouble, for the forces trying to bring peace in Afghanistan.

Although most observers in Europe and America were worried about the extension of local control and the establishment of sharia courts, some commentators in Pakistan thought the change was a good idea. They claimed that the official legal system, inherited from the British, was unworkable. There were few judges and lawyers trained in the British system. Traditional sharia law was what the local people wanted, they claimed. They said it would be better to have some system of law and order than an unworkable system.

However, the local Taliban destroyed girls' schools in the region. Their own councils announced that they would decide whether or not to reopen any of them. In at least one incident, the local Taliban militia kidnapped and held Pakistani government officials in Mingora, the main town in Swat. The Taliban leaders said that the cease-fire with Pakistani troops would not go into effect until the government removed all of their troops from the region.

It seemed that the Taliban and their allies were taking over various regions, either formally or informally, in the troubled border zone. The development of strengthened local control did not seem to many U.S. and European observers like the way to stop the raids by Taliban and al-Qaeda forces into Afghanistan. Instead, it seemed that Pakistan had only made it easier to establish sanctuaries or safe havens for Afghan Taliban.

Others claimed that the Pakistani Taliban was very different from the Afghan Taliban, and that the Pakistani Taliban did not like the presence of al-Qaeda and foreign fighters in their tribal agencies. Some thought that if the local Pakistani Taliban were left alone, they would help control the Afghans and al-Qaeda among them. The Pakistani president said strong local leaders could stop al-Qaeda raids into Afghanistan. But from the outside, it was very difficult to tell who was right.

Thousands of refugees began fleeing from Swat in 2009 because of the strict enforcement of sharia by the local Taliban. Furthermore, the

U.S. Army soldiers and Afghanistan National Army soldiers meet local villagers in an effort to locate caves where al-Qaeda or Taliban personnel might be hiding along the Afghan-Pakistani border. *(Department of Defense)*

Taliban arrested representatives of the Pakistani government. In May 2009, the Pakistani government responded by sending in a large force of troops to expel the Taliban from control of Swat and to arrest the Taliban leaders there.

The U.S. military believed that the Pakistani government either would not or could not track down and arrest the al-Qaeda and Taliban leaders. So U.S. forces attacked some of the suspected training camps and residences of those leaders directly. Instead of flying in with manned aircraft or using missiles from offshore ships, the U.S. forces began to use small unmanned aircraft. Most well-known of these aircraft was the Predator drone.

Predator drones have television cameras to identify targets on the ground. They can be fired so that small missiles destroy buildings or other sites, sometimes killing terrorists. There were 10 announced attacks in 2006 and 2007.

The number of air strikes increased to 36 in 2008. The rate further increased in 2009, after the new administration of Barack Obama took office. Some of the attacks on South Waziristan were in the region controlled by the local Taliban leader Baitullah Mehsud; some were in an area controlled by a rival leader, Mullah Nazir. Nazir was reportedly wounded in one of the 2008 missile attacks.

In a number of small incidents, U.S. ground forces pursuing Taliban and al-Qaeda fighters chased them across the ill-defined border into Pakistan. On September 15 and 22, 2008, Pakistani troops fired on U.S. helicopters. The Pakistanis said that the helicopters had crossed over the border into Pakistan. The episodes did not attract much worldwide attention, but they showed how dangerous the situation could become. Neither the United States nor Pakistan wanted to go to war. Even so, many people in Pakistan were very angry at the United States.

In the United States, President Barack Obama took office on January 20, 2009. Following up on his position that the war in Afghanistan was more important and more legitimate than the war in Iraq, he appointed a special ambassador, Richard Holbrooke, to deal with the joint problem of Afghanistan and Pakistan. In fact, the American press began to name the new approach the AFPAK policy.

Whether or not Mr. Holbrooke would be able to get the Pakistani government to cooperate more effectively in tracking down and arresting or killing the criminals of al-Qaeda would be a major issue facing the new American president.

WEAPONS AND TACTICS

The history of Afghanistan haunted the officers and enlisted men in the international forces, including the Americans, who sought to bring peace to the country in the period following the overthrow of the Taliban in early 2002. The British had tried to conquer Afghanistan in 1842 and 1878 but did not succeed. And, as explained in chapter 3, the Soviet Union had tried to take over Afghanistan from 1979 to 1989. Afghanistan is known as the graveyard of empires.

Afghanistan is difficult to conquer and control because of the weapons and tactics used by Afghan warriors. Traditionally, bands of irregular soldiers, operating under local leaders—known variously as tribal chiefs, warlords, generals, or commanders—had resisted control not only by outsiders but by any central government. They had a unique, Afghan way of war, with methods well adapted to defeat large organized armies through the use of irregular or insurgent forces.

The reasons that the country was so easily thrown into military chaos and was so hard to control from a central capital were straightforward enough. Large strategic, geographic, and international factors help explain the Afghan choice of weapons and tactics.

The rugged countryside, with mountain valleys blocked by snow in the winter and only primitive roads into many regions, meant that large armies, even modern ones equipped with armored vehicles and helicopters, found it difficult to establish control in remote regions. Local irregulars or guerrilla fighters, often equipped only with old rifles, could ambush regular troops, whether an Afghan army from the central government or outsiders like the British, Russians, and Americans.

Because Afghanistan is at the crossroads of empires, caught between the powerful neighboring states of Iran to the west, Pakistan to the east

Members of the Afghanistan Military Forces (AMF), armed with British Enfield rifles, sit alongside the road and watch as Coalition forces pass by in March 2002. Afghan soldiers such as these had supported the Coalition in driving out the Taliban. *(Department of Defense)*

and south, and Russia and China to the north and east, there have always been one or more outside countries willing to provide weapons or safe havens to one or more factions inside the country. Those factors, combined with the mountainous landscape, have favored the local irregulars over the regular armies that have tried to conquer them.

With powerful, rival states on every border, the irregular fighters have used imported weapons, smuggled in from friends over the borders, and weapons and explosives that they have captured from the forces trying to control them. For this reason, the fighters have always had a mixed assortment of weapons, such as old British Enfield .303 rifles, Russian Kalashnikov AK-47 machine guns, and American M-1 and M-15 rifles. When the CIA first provided assistance to the mujahideen against the Soviets in the 1980s, they went to some trouble to shop around the world for used Enfield rifles and used and captured Soviet equipment so that the support could not be traced to the United States.

Small groups of Afghan fighters, often less than 20 and rarely more than 100, would operate independently under the command of a single leader. Only rarely would such small bands group together into larger

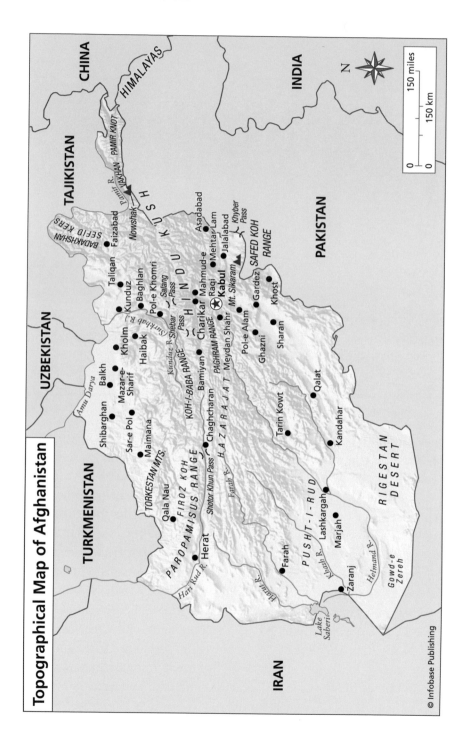

Topographical Map of Afghanistan

© Infobase Publishing

units. When the highly organized and large armies of invaders like the British or Russians sought to engage the Afghans in battle, they would only encounter small independent units. Captured Afghan irregulars could not provide any intelligence about the other bands, simply because they really operated completely independently of each other.

SOVIET TACTICS

Soviet tactics called for staying more than 300 meters (985 ft) away from the enemy. The mujahideen fired rifles and shoulder-launched anti-tank grenades in a line of sight, with the range of such weapons usually limited to about 300 meters. If the Soviet forces could maintain a long distance to the enemy, it would give an advantage to the Soviets, who could fire at much longer ranges from their tanks and artillery in a ballistic arc rather than in a flat trajectory.

The mujahideen would take cover in orchards, in small villages, or in rocky country, and the Soviets would try to clear all such cover 300 meters on each side of roads, so that their weapons would have an advantage. While the method worked, it meant that much of the crops, homes, villages, and other structures in the countryside had to be destroyed.

These two Soviet tanks resting in a field near Bagram Air Base are among the many such pieces of military hardware that litter Afghanistan, reminders of the decades of warfare that have ravaged this country. (*Department of Defense*)

SOVIET ARMOR IN AFGHANISTAN

The Soviets brought many heavy armored vehicles into Afghanistan during their war. Among the armored vehicles they brought were heavy T-55, T-62, and T-72 tanks and the BMP-2. The BMP (*Boyevaya Mashina Pekhoty*) was a tracked vehicle used to transport ammunition and fuel. Many were destroyed by rocket-propelled grenades, made more effective by the hazardous and easily detonated cargoes of the BMPs. When U.S. troops encountered BMPs that had survived and were now in the hands of the Taliban, they called them "Bimps." The Soviet vehicles mounting antiaircraft guns, ZSU-23s, when later taken over by the Taliban, would be parked on a hill so that their weapons could be leveled at attacking troops. U.S. Special Forces troops called them "Zeuses."

Russian heavy wheeled vehicles included the BTR-70 and BTR-80. These transporters were used in convoys to move troops and equipment. All of these heavy pieces of equipment did not work very well in Afghanistan's terrain, and they tended to reduce the mobility of troops. They might have been suited to a large-scale engagement with armored forces from NATO countries if there had ever been a ground clash of forces between the Soviets and the U.S. allies in Europe. But in Afghanistan, such equipment simply provided targets for the more mobile mujahideen. Nevertheless, the surviving heavy armor in the hands of the Taliban and the Northern Alliance troops supplemented the lighter weapons used by Afghan soldiers on both sides in 2001 and 2002.

The tactics that the irregular fighters use in Afghanistan have not varied much over the decades. Usually using only small weapons that they can carry or that they can move by mules or horses—rifles, light machine guns, explosives, and shoulder-held rocket launchers—they have been able to stand off much more heavily equipped forces. The Soviets learned how difficult it was to fight the Afghans in the 1980s.

The Soviets tried to establish control relying on heavy artillery and armored vehicles with some close air support from jets and helicopters. As long as the Soviet troops could clear an area of several hundred yards around a particular point, they could defend it against the mujahideen equipped with rifles and light machine guns. Using heavy artillery guns, the Soviets could defend a perimeter or circle around a specific point against almost any attack by the mujahideen. With helicopters and aircraft for surveillance, the Soviets could detect the movements

One member of a U.S. Army team holds a Stinger missile, while the other scans the horizon for incoming aircraft. Although this is only a training exercise, it demonstrates the way that the mujahideen were able to employ the Stinger to shoot down Soviet aircraft. *(Department of Defense)*

of large numbers of mujahideen and be ready for them at their own defended points. However, this Soviet use of artillery for defending static points made it difficult to take the offensive and move into mountain regions where the mujahideen moved freely about. Their heavy armored vehicles made movement on main roads somewhat easier, but they were easy targets for handheld weapons by the mujahideen.

Furthermore, the mujahideen never wore specific uniforms. In their traditional civilian clothing, if they were chased into villages they would simply blend into the local population. When the Soviets moved on, the mujahideen would reassemble, recruit some new young boys to join them, and be ready for another battle. One of the traditional methods of such small bands of fighters was to put the most enthusiastic and least experienced young recruits in the front of any sudden assault. If they were killed, wounded, or captured, the commanders would simply abandon them on the field and let the foreign enemy take care of the prisoners or dispose of the bodies. The hardened and experienced fighters would retreat to make new recruits and fight again.

Another traditional aspect of how Afghans fought was very confusing to all of the outsiders who came in to try to control the country.

When one Afghan unit was fighting another unit, as when competing mujahideen groups fought each other or when insurgents fought
against Afghan government troops, the battles would often end very
strangely from the point of view of foreigners like the British, Russians, or Americans. When one Afghan commander saw that his fighters were going to lose against another Afghan commander, he would
negotiate a surrender.

Often the surrendering fighters would be given the option of going
home or joining the winning side. This courteous treatment was not
extended to foreigners, whether they were British, Russian, American,
or even the Arab foreign fighters who later came in to fight with al-
Qaeda against the U.S.-led coalition. When foreign soldiers were captured by Afghans, the foreigners, wounded or not, would be tortured
and killed rather than taken prisoner.

Because the United States sought to throw the Soviets out of
Afghanistan in the 1980s, American forces sent modern shoulder-held

THE STINGER

The Stinger was first introduced to the U.S. weapons arsenal in 1987.
The weapon is five feet long, with a firing tube five and a half inches in
diameter. Fully armed, the weapon weighs under 35 pounds, so it can
be readily carried by one man, although a two-man crew is required to
load and launch the missile. Despite its small size, it has a range of up
to eight kilometers (about five miles) and could hit low-flying jets and
helicopters up to 10,000 feet in altitude.

The system is known as a "fire and forget" weapon, because it is
self-guided with an infrared heat-seeker system. Between 900 and
1,200 Stingers were supplied to the mujahideen during their resistance
to the Soviet occupation in the late 1980s. The missile was made under
a prime contract with Hughes Missile System Company, with General
Dynamics/Raytheon Corporation engaged in the actual production. The
replacement cost for one missile during the period of deployment was
$38,000.

Some journalists credited the Stinger with the decision of the
Soviets to withdraw from Afghanistan, although the decision probably
had far more to do with the high rate of ground casualties and growing
discontent within the Soviet Union over the long-drawn-out conflict in
Afghanistan over the period from 1979 to 1989.

antiaircraft rockets through Pakistan to various units of the mujahideen, at first through secret funding and later more openly. The most famous of these weapons imported and used by the mujahideen against the Soviets was the Stinger antiaircraft rocket. Using heat-seeking direction guidance, the rockets would home in on the heat of a Soviet helicopter or jet engine.

With the defeat of the Soviets and their retreat from Afghanistan in 1989, the Soviet-supported Communist regime tried to maintain control. But as was traditional in Afghanistan, local forces resisted control from a central government.

Then, out of the chaotic conditions, the Taliban militants came in and established control over the capital and most of the country's provinces in 1995. However, as with previous central governments, the Taliban government never established full control over the nation. Mujahideen armies, particularly those based among the Uzbek and Tajik groups of the North, fought against the Taliban who were mostly Pashtun people from the south and east of the country. The Northern Alliance units were organized a bit differently than the traditional Afghan bands. Operating under generals with staff officers and a regular chain of command, with companies organized into regiments and divisions, the Northern Alliance fielded troops that seemed more like the armies of Western countries.

The Northern Alliance forces had some leftover armored vehicles, including tanks that the Soviets had left behind. Although many had been damaged or left behind after breakdowns, Northern Alliance mechanics were able to get a small number of the tanks operable, and they used them against Taliban troops.

After the Taliban sheltered Osama bin Laden and the United States presented an ultimatum to the Taliban government following the 9/11 attacks of 2001, the Northern Alliance of mujahideen armies received sudden support from the United States and then from NATO forces in their effort to throw out the Taliban. Once again, as throughout Afghan history, insurgent irregular forces sought and received aid from powerful outsiders.

In addition to support from airpower, small units of U.S. and British Special Forces were air-dropped into the country, bringing small hand-held equipment. Included were GPS devices similar to those used in cars. Working in very small units of less than 10, these men would cooperate with larger Northern Alliance bands and armies. When Taliban forces could be identified, either in a specific location or in vehicles, the Special Forces would radio for air support. U.S. and British jets, flying in from aircraft carriers and from bases in Pakistan and Uzbekistan, would identify the ground targets, from GPS coordinates. Sometimes, the men on the ground would mark the targets with lasers, and the aircraft would drop the smart bombs on their precise locations. These targeting teams and their special equipment proved to be crucial to the rapid success of the Northern Alliance over the Taliban in early 2002.

This combination of modern, high-technology fighting with the traditional method of warfare and leftover Soviet equipment contributed to the rapid collapse of the Taliban army in late 2001 and early 2002. Although regular U.S. and NATO troops came in to support the Northern Alliance, the Northern Alliance troops succeeded in capturing Kabul and most of the country's major cities. The traditional Afghan tactic of surrendering and switching sides also helps account for the rather quick victory of the Northern Alliance against the Taliban government in 2002, as some Taliban soldiers would surrender and switch sides to join the winning Northern Alliance. But the Northern Alliance did not accept al-Qaeda foreign fighters into their ranks, and they fled from the advancing troops rather than face battlefield torture and execution.

U.S. soldiers were surprised at another Afghan tactic. The soldiers under Northern Alliance general Abdul Rashid Dostum fired their weapons very strangely. They would hold an automatic rifle such as a Kalishnikov high over their heads and "spray and pray" as the GIs said. They did not aim at the enemy. When asked why, they explained that if an enemy was killed, it was God's will, not because they had taken careful aim.

In contrast to the lightly armed Afghan troops who carried little besides a weapon, ammunition, and water, American foot soldiers in Afghanistan were weighed down by 80 to 100 pounds of equipment. In addition to a weapon and its ammunition, water, bedroll, ground cloth, uniform, body armor, and helmet, Americans typically packed night-vision equipment, a change of underwear, soap, toothpaste, a notebook and pen, a compass, food bars, and other items. Much of the supplies and equipment would be in a backpack or waist pack that also weighed a few pounds. Radiomen, medics, and squad leaders had even more to carry. The equipment, body armor, and uniform tended to rapidly exhaust soldiers working in 100-degree heat.

When Osama bin Laden and his group of al-Qaeda supporters took refuge in the cave complex near the Pakistani border in the Tora Bora region, heavy bombing of the caves from aircraft combined with ground operations was intended to destroy their hideouts. U.S. C-130 cargo aircraft dropped several heavy Daisy Cutter bombs in the Tora Bora region. Their huge mushroom clouds spurred false rumors that the U.S. forces had used nuclear weapons. Even so, the combined attack with ground forces and attack from the air only led to the escape of most of the al-Qaeda leadership over the mountain ranges into Pakistan, where, as far as the outside world is aware, the al-Qaeda core leadership has continued to hide.

Using satellite surveillance and surveillance from drone aircraft over the years, U.S. forces have continued to identify specific al-Qaeda individuals and small groups in Pakistan. After identification, an armed Predator drone has been sent in, targeting the individuals or groups. The use of this intelligence-gathering and weapons system has some advantages from a political point of view. Since no human pilots have to be over Pakistani territory, the attacks do not quite represent an invasion of Pakistan.

There is always a gap in time between when the information was gathered and when the strike takes place, sometimes leading to mistakes such as blowing up an empty house or killing innocent civilians. The al-Qaeda leaders often hide in populated areas, knowing that the Americans want to avoid incidents that lead to the death and wounding of innocents. So the political advantage of not actually sending any personnel into Pakistan is offset by the negative effect of the civilian deaths that can be attributed to the U.S. drone raids.

Meanwhile, the Taliban and al-Qaeda forces continue to resist the establishment of a central government in Afghanistan, using some of the traditional methods of hit-and-run attacks. As in earlier wars, Afghan irregulars operated with lightly armed forces, sabotage of infrastructure, such as bombing bridges, schools, electrical-generating facilities, water supplies, and planting roadside bombs. Improvised explosive devices (IEDs) often consist of a jug of explosive or a wired artillery shell and are planted in or next to roads, then detonated when U.S., ISAF, or Afghan troops or police are passing by in a vehicle.

Because there is no widespread cell phone network in Afghanistan, the IEDs are usually not detonated by a wireless phone call. Rather, more are hardwired with either a pressure plate in the road to make the

THE PREDATOR

The Predator unmanned aerial vehicle (UAV) has a wingspan of 48.7 feet and is 27 feet long, while the Predator B is slightly larger at 66 feet long with a 36-foot wingspan. The aircraft was first developed with radar and television cameras for spotting targets and movements on the ground. However, later models were armed with Hellfire missiles, which allows the unmanned aircraft to be used to strike remote targets without endangering the lives of pilots.

The first Predator was test-flown in 1994, and they were regularly produced beginning in 1997. The U.S. Air Force employed them extensively in Bosnia, and they have been used in Afghanistan. The U.S. government does not officially comment on reports of Predator strikes within Pakistan. But it is widely known that numerous Predator strikes, using the advanced MQ9 Reaper Hunter/Killer models firing missiles, have been used against identified al-Qaeda and Taliban camps and hideouts in Pakistan.

There were 10 identified strikes in 2007 and more than 30 in 2008, with the strikes continuing at a high rate in 2009 and 2010. The small unmanned aircraft can carry Hellfire antiarmor missiles and laser-guided bombs. Because its television and radar signals are relayed by satellite, it can be operated in the field from anywhere in the world.

electrical contact or with wires running to a remote location where an observer sets off the explosion as target vehicles pass by. In response to these devices, U.S. forces have imported the heavily armored mine protected clearance vehicles (MPCVs), the Buffalos described in chapter 1.

Traveling in convoys, led by mine-detecting and mine-clearing vehicles, troops and equipment are moved by truck and armored personnel carrier even into remote regions. However, the ISAF and U.S. forces, with their heavy equipment, have to move very carefully and deliberately. To the extent that they use this convoy method, they seem to fall into the same traps that defeated the Soviets. As always, the traditional insurgent method of warfare with quick hit-and-run strikes by lightly armed ground forces on foot or traveling on horseback continued to thwart efforts to bring peace to the country.

In addition, Afghan insurgents have imported a tactic developed by Palestinians against Israeli government forces (and even earlier by

Reports leaked out that the strikes had some important successes. In 2008, at least five major leaders of either the Taliban or al-Qaeda were killed. Attacks in North and South Waziristan and in Bajaur in Pakistan's Federally Administered Tribal Areas succeeded. The head of al-Qaeda's military forces in tribal areas, the leader of the al-Qaeda weapons of mass destruction program, as well as others were confirmed casualties of the Predator attacks. However, local leaders complained that some of the strikes also killed innocent family members or others nearby and that the Predator strikes represented violations of Pakistan's sovereignty.

A U.S. Air Force Predator drone armed with a missile and controlled by an air force pilot in Nevada taxis down the runway at an air base in Iraq. *(Department of Defense)*

Tamil rebels against the government of Sri Lanka): the use of suicide bombers who wear a vest loaded with explosives. Finding a crowded location, such as a market, a city transit bus, or a mosque, the suicide bomber will detonate his vest, often killing and wounding dozens of innocent bystanders as well as himself. Such a weapon is usually not effective against troops, as they are careful not to gather in large, easily targeted groups. However, suicide bombers, with their tragic destruction of innocent bystanders, help demonstrate that a government lacks firm control over a country.

Gradually over the years of combat in both Iraq and Afghanistan, U.S. and allied forces have learned a great deal about counterinsurgency operations. Faced with the Afghans' traditional method of warfare, U.S. commanders have come to realize that they cannot simply expect to establish control and hold points, using superior armored forces. Heavy, slow-moving equipment may provide protection to the troops, but it is not flexible and rapid enough to track down and identify the irregular Afghan fighters using their traditional methods.

Instead, U.S. and allied forces had to develop and use small units, working closely with local troops and police to serve as guides and interpreters. After chasing a Taliban band into a remote region, close

AFGHANISTAN WAR'S DISTINCTIVE PROFILE

Unlike most wars throughout history, the war in Afghanistan has not involved large forces of combatants squaring off against one another. Instead, the war has involved battles that are more like firefights, where small units engage briefly, or operations, which go on for many days with only occasional contact between enemy forces. The reason is that, with a few exceptions, irregulars like the Taliban deliberately adopt the strategy of avoiding major engagements. This list of some of the so-called battles and operations in Afghanistan illustrates this point.

Takur Ghar: *March 3–4, 2003:* During Operation Anaconda, its most devastating battle occurred at Takur Ghar, a mountain peak in the region, where the U.S. forces attempted to set up an observation post. In the futile battle that ensued, two U.S. helicopters were shot down and two U.S. SEALs were lost.

Now Zad: *March 2006–October 2009:* Now Zad (or Nawzad) is the capital city of a district in Helmand Province where the Taliban has continued to be a constant threat. British troops were first assigned to defend Now Zad; they were later joined by Estonians. In March 2008, U.S. Marines took over and, after frequent engagements, they succeeded in driving the insurgents out of Now Zad. But as of January 2010, the marines continued to face heavy opposition in the surrounding district.

Operation Mountain Thrust: *May 15–July 31, 2006:* This was one of the largest operations of the war, involving 2,300 U.S., 3,300 UK, 2,200 Canadian, and 3,500 Afghan soldiers. Its objective was to quell the Taliban insurgency in southern Afghanistan, but it had only limited results.

Operation Achilles: *March 6–May 30, 2007:* In the largest NATO operation to date, troops went into Helmand Province, a Taliban stronghold, and engaged in a series of encounters that left 35

work with local residents was required to identify the enemy fighters and then to capture or kill them one by one. Unless the local residents could be confident that the U.S. troops and their colleagues from the Afghan army were going to stay and maintain order, they would hesitate to reveal who among them were fighters hiding out.

NATO troops dead; estimates of Taliban dead ranged from 750 to 2,000.

Musa Qala: *October 12, 2008:* The Taliban seized Musa Qala, an important market town in northern Helmand Province. Occupied by the British since December 10, 2007, Musa Qala had been the scene of constant attacks by the Taliban.

Operation Khanjar (or Strike of the Sword): *July 2, 2009:* In the largest airlift of marines since the Vietnam War, some 4,000 were flown into Helmand Province to commence what would be an ongoing operation both to drive out the Taliban and to remain on the ground to support the local populace.

Dahaneh: *August 12–15, 2009:* Dahaneh, a town in Helmand Province, was controlled by the Taliban since 2005. After four days of fighting, U.S. and Afghan troops drove out the Taliban.

A U.S. airman in a C-130 is dropping a box of 10,000 leaflets over the mountains of southeastern Afghanistan. The leaflets carry a message aimed at Taliban extremists, warning them of the consequences if they interfere with Coalition operations in this region. *(Department of Defense)*

Counterinsurgency tactics, to be effective, cannot simply rely on airpower and heavy equipment. Instead, they have to rely on good intelligence, cooperation and confidence-building with local leadership, and sometimes a house-by-house method that involves identifying and capturing the enemy one by one. They also require staying in a neighborhood or village in sufficient numbers and long enough to establish local law and order.

It is not the high-technology weapons or the superiority of airpower and armor that wins, but the "weapons" of close cooperation with and training of local forces and methods that border on law enforcement rather than military field operations. These methods include careful interrogation, sifting of evidence, and arrest and detention of "bad guys." The method also requires sufficient numbers of troops to be effective in driving enemy bands into cornered positions.

Because the Taliban fighters threaten the host family with whom they are hiding out, it is hard to identify the insurgent troops when they melt into the countryside. An irregular Taliban fighter will tell a family that if they turn him in to the U.S. or British troops, his comrades will come by and rape the women and children of the host family and torture and kill the adult men. Faced with such threats, local families often refuse to identify the Taliban fighters hiding among them. Only if they are confident that the U.S. soldiers and the Afghan authorities are strong enough and numerous enough to offer protection and remain in control of the local region will they dare to identify specific Taliban fighters who are pretending to be innocent members of the family or village. The tactic of intimidation can only be defeated by establishing control and confidence.

The adjustment to the special needs of counterinsurgency in Afghanistan has been very difficult, not only for the U.S. troops, but for the other outside countries that have participated. One approach has been a weapon of psychological warfare called PSYOPs, techniques used to win over local support through a wide variety of methods. Under the International Security Assistance Force (ISAF), numerous provincial reconstruction teams (PRTs) have been established.

The PRTs are run and staffed by troops and advisers from a wide variety of countries (including large numbers from Germany and smaller numbers from Switzerland and Belgium). They engage in activities designed to improve security and to help reconstruct facilities in Afghanistan. The goal is not only reconstruction but confidence-

U.S. Army general Stanley A. McChrystal, pictured here as a brigadier general, was a lieutenant general when in May 2009 he was appointed to command the U.S. forces in Afghanistan and also the International Security Assistance Force (ISAF) there. *(Department of Defense)*

building in the Afghan government and attempting to win over the "hearts and minds" of the population.

In Kunduz Province, for example, a German-run PRT engages in small local projects such as repairs to a police station and digging of wells, as well as producing regular publications and radio broadcasts to help support the Afghan government. Other PRTs run clinics and health-education programs and engage in local projects to help rebuild the country. For many of the countries providing assistance through the ISAF, the military forces work strictly in such civilian reconstruction projects, rather than in direct combat roles.

Many of the ISAF countries have concentrated their efforts in trying to build cooperation and support with local leaders by establishing schools, clinics, building roads and bridges, training police, and restoring power and water supplies. While such aid projects do bring some benefits to the local people, they also have the drawback of providing new targets for the Taliban forces to attack. Schools, clinics, power stations, police stations, and other recently built structures and offices can be readily identified and damaged or destroyed. So the PSYOPs weapon has not always been as effective as planners hoped.

As President Obama transferred the focus of U.S. military effort to Afghanistan, he made a concerted effort not only to provide more troops but to bring a change in the leadership of troops on the ground. In May 2009, the U.S. Department of Defense appointed Lieutenant General Stanley A. McChrystal to take command of U.S. forces in Afghanistan.

With background and experience in counterinsurgency in Iraq, McChrystal took over from the four-star General David McKiernan, whose background was in traditional conventional warfare that relied on the movement of armor and heavy forces against regular armies. It was the first replacement of a U.S. four-star general in the field in time of war since Harry Truman dismissed General Douglas MacArthur during the Korean War in 1951. It was hoped that the new approach, with greater emphasis on counterinsurgency tactics, would finally bring peace to Afghanistan.

THE ROAD AHEAD

As Obama's presidency entered its first few months in 2009, the major foreign issue facing the new president was the ongoing war in Afghanistan. Like other members of his party, Obama had criticized the former administration for its conduct of both the war in Iraq and the war in Afghanistan.

Similarly to Massachusetts senator John Kerry, Obama had held that the war in Afghanistan had been neglected. Compared to the war in Iraq, the Afghan war was seen as a "good" war, justified precisely because Afghanistan had harbored Osama bin Laden, who had financed and organized the attacks on the United States on 9/11. Like Senator Kerry, Obama believed that the efforts spent in Iraq were misguided and that more effort, money, resources, and troops should have been devoted to winning the war in Afghanistan. Obama said that peace in Afghanistan was important to the peace in the whole region.

Obama honored his campaign commitment to send more troops to Afghanistan, bringing the total of U.S. forces in that country to about 60,000 by late summer 2009, with the total planned to increase to 68,000 by the end of the year. He later announced an increase to about 100,000 by midyear 2010. Nevertheless, the question remained: Would the forces be enough to establish peace in Afghanistan? Furthermore, since the American public already seemed impatient to bring both the Iraq War and the Afghanistan War to conclusions, some observers predicted that Afghanistan would represent a major crisis for the new president. Some argued that the war was simply not winnable.

Considering the history of Afghanistan summarized in this volume, there are a lot of reasons for this pessimistic view. Local Afghan forces drove out both the British Empire (in the 19th century) and the Soviet Union (in the 20th century). Afghanistan is known as the graveyard of empires.

U.S. Army general David Petraeus, here testifying before the Senate Armed Services Committee in April 2009, was named in October 2008 to command the U.S. Central Command. In this position, he became responsible for overseeing U.S. operations in both Iraq and Afghanistan. *(Department of Defense)*

Afghanistan's rugged mountain terrain with high mountain valleys and passes impossible to cross in winter always favored local forces. Indigenous fighters who could blend into the population had a natural advantage over heavily equipped outsiders. As the Russian troops learned during the Soviet occupation in the 1980s, modern heavy equipment designed for a land war in Europe against other well-equipped armies was ill suited to the situation in Afghanistan.

The linguistic and cultural differences of the different groups that make up Afghanistan had always made it difficult for a central government to rule effectively. Even though severely divided among themselves, Afghans had usually united around one issue: They hated the idea of foreign domination and foreigners telling them how to run their country.

Because of these factors, the country for centuries has been dominated by local warlords who rely on long-standing warrior traditions. This meant that whenever a strong central government tried to take over, with or without the aid of outside armies, local chiefs, clan leaders, and military leaders could appeal to young men in their neighborhood

AFGHANISTAN AND ITS NEIGHBORS

Afghanistan has always reacted strongly to the policies of its neighboring countries. In the 21st century, this factor was as important as it had been in the past. The 1,500-mile border with Pakistan, running right through areas occupied by Pashtun people on both sides of the line, has been very important. The other neighbors are important as well.

To the west of Afghanistan is the Islamic Republic of Iran, dominated by a religiously governed regime, in which a clerical council has to approve any candidates for office. On June 12, 2009, Iran held its 10th presidential election, and the government declared incumbent Mahmoud Ahmadinejad the winner over the protests of hundreds of thousands of demonstrators. Ahmadinejad was strongly anti-American and defended the country's right to develop nuclear weapons. Iran shares with Afghanistan a 580-mile border, and Iran has always dabbled in internal Afghanistan politics, supporting Shia and radical political parties and armed mujahideen groups.

Just to the north of Afghanistan lies the former Soviet republic of Uzbekistan, sharing a border that is about 85 miles long. In the first years of Operation Enduring Freedom, Uzbekistan provided air-landing areas and passage for U.S. troops into Afghanistan. In July 2005, the Uzbeks terminated the agreement with the United States and evicted the United States from its air base after the United States criticized the Uzbek government for its brutal suppression of an uprising. However, relations gradually improved after 2007. Then in April 2009, Uzbekistan once again agreed to let the United States ship goods into Afghanistan from airfields in Uzbekistan.

The People's Republic of China shares only a very small border with Afghanistan—about 47 miles. This short border is in the extreme northeast of Afghanistan. Even so, China has watched developments in Afghanistan very carefully. China frowned on the development of an extreme Islamist state in Afghanistan under the Taliban. The Chinese government is concerned about unrest among Islamic minorities within China itself and thus worries that radical Islamism in Afghanistan could affect its own domestic peace.

Thus, the outcome of events in Afghanistan has been dependent on the positions of the neighboring countries. And the outcome of events in Afghanistan will have a great impact on those same neighboring countries. For that reason, the Obama administration has hoped that other countries in the region will offer more cooperation in bringing stability to the country.

or region to pick up arms and join a rebellion. Such a rebellion by the mujahideen threw out the Soviets in 1989.

The Communist government left behind by the Soviets was thrown out by the Taliban in 1996. And between 2001 and 2002, the dictatorial Taliban was itself overthrown by the Northern Alliance with aid from the United States and Great Britain. It seems that the cycle of resistance to a central government works against any effort by anyone, insider or outsider, to bring stability to the country.

Still other factors suggest that Obama will not face an easy task to end the war in Afghanistan. The Taliban and al-Qaeda forces that resisted U.S. and NATO forces have safe havens across the border in Pakistan. Although the Pakistani government has attempted to root out the centers of Taliban influence and control in the border regions, the connections between local commanders and the anti-American and anti-NATO forces in Afghanistan remain strong.

The Pashtun people in Pakistan's border areas, as in Afghanistan, have a long tradition of protecting any fugitives from outside officials who came in to arrest them. It was the Pashtunwali—the code of honor that called for hospitality to guests—that protected renegades, smugglers, criminals, rebels, and other fugitives from authority.

Because the United States did not want to offend the Pakistani government and people by sending troops into Pakistan, the United States tried to attack Taliban and al-Qaeda strongholds with the Predator drones. This remotely operated, pilotless aircraft could deliver bombs with great accuracy on particular buildings, vehicles, or even individuals.

The strikes increased in 2009 and 2010, but it was difficult to assess their success or failure. Furthermore, even though no U.S. ground troops or pilots were involved inside Pakistan, the drone strikes tend to build resentment among Pakistanis. Such air strikes sometimes resulted in collateral damage. That is, sometimes the missiles accidentally hit and killed or wounded completely innocent civilians in tragic mistakes.

Nevertheless, with the increased numbers of Predator attacks, some victories were achieved, such as the death in August 2009 of Baitullah Mehsud, the Pakistani Taliban leader who had led the cooperation with Afghan Taliban from Pakistan. Continued reports later in August 2009 of an internal struggle for power among the Pakistani Taliban, with shootouts, assassinations, and a pitched battle near the village of Sura

Ghar with rockets and mortars, suggested that the Taliban there was in no condition to provide aid to the Afghan Taliban.

In Afghanistan, other local factors worked against a quick, peaceful solution. With the disruption of the economy by decades of war, almost the only export crop or commodity that Afghans could sell to other countries was opium. Opium grown in Afghanistan represented about 90 percent of the world's source for illegal heroin. Although the profits from the opium trade went to traders and smugglers outside of Afghanistan, there were still large amounts of illegal money flowing into the country from this export crop.

As a consequence of the flow of money from organized crime, drug dealers would bribe local, provincial, and central government officials and military officers to ignore the drug trade. Corruption remains a major problem. Honest Afghans had little faith in their government, and that faith was reduced even more as they heard about drug dealing, bribery, corrupt officials, and paid-off police and army officers.

An Afghanistan National Auxiliary Police officer salutes at a basic training course graduation ceremony in February 2008. The Afghanistan government initiated the auxiliary police program to supplement efforts of the National Police Force to maintain security. *(Department of Defense)*

As British, U.S., and other Western army personnel tried to train Afghan civilians to serve as policemen or as soldiers in the central government's army, they found they had a very hard job. Many of the young Afghan recruits had never been to school and did not have experience learning from a teacher. Most of them had no understanding of the concept of human rights, let alone the rights of women. If they were issued a gun, they might sell it and claim it was stolen. The black market price of weapons represented a great temptation.

Afghan support for a central government has always been weak. Whenever the central government appointed a provincial governor or other local official, unless that appointee had strong local family and clan ties, he would be resented and sometimes killed. So President Hamid Karzai faced a difficult choice. He could appoint people loyal to him—and win the opposition of local folk. Or he could appoint a local leader with strong local ties—but then that administrator would really owe no political debt or loyalty to Karzai or to the central government.

As if these problems were not severe enough, the country continued to be troubled by extreme hostility between Shia and Sunni branches of Islam, with some government officials using their power to try to stamp out any evidence of Shia or Iranian influence. Some also tried to suppress the use of the Dari language, spoken by Afghans in western Afghanistan. Dari, similar to the Farsi spoken in Iran, seemed to militant Pashtun and Sunni government officials as a symptom of subversive Iranian influence.

The contrast between the troubled situation in Afghanistan and that in Iraq was not promising. Although the war in Iraq had dragged on for years, by 2009, it seemed that progress toward stability had arrived. However, it seems unlikely that a similar stability will come to Afghanistan.

Iraq was a much more modern country. Even though Saddam Hussein was a ruthless dictator, Iraq was somewhat prosperous under his regime. There were modern highways, buildings, shopping centers, and suburbs, well served by public utilities such as power lines and water supplies. Iraq had a good source of international money in the form of oil exports. In Iraq, there was a large, educated professional and middle class. Large numbers of women had careers in business, government, education, and medicine. None of those features were present in Afghanistan, which remains one of the poorest countries in the world.

In contrast to Iraq, Afghanistan does not seem a likely candidate for a democratic government in the style of Western democracies like those of Europe and North America. Such democracies require certain social and traditional factors. They need to have a large middle class, an educated population, and a tradition of relying on the rule of law in which private enterprise can flourish. They need to have social stability, in which religious and ethnic differences are somehow peacefully managed and resolved. *None* of these factors or traditions are present in Afghanistan. So the hopes that a democratic, central regime, supported by U.S. and NATO troops, would bring peace to the country seemed to be working against the facts.

Another worrying sign in Afghanistan was the emergence of a strong, second in command under Mullah Omar as leader of the Afghan Taliban. Mullah Abdul Ghani Baradar, although he always deferred to Omar as the supreme leader, commanded the forces on the ground. Baradar was noted for his efficient control, bringing together the disorganized Afghan Taliban, and for his use of modern technology, including the Internet, satellite telephones, and motorcycles. He demanded accurate reports, backed up by video camera footage, of every attack on Americans. Taliban troops would receive cash bounties for the numbers of Americans they could report killed, carefully and accurately assigned by Baradar. He paid them with money still flowing from rich supporters of al-Qaeda and the Taliban in some of the oil-exporting nations.

In 2009, another worrying sign was that casualties among British and U.S. troops climbed to the highest numbers of the whole war. The Taliban's roadside bombs continued to take a toll on lives. General Stanley McChrystal warned that U.S. casualties were running at record levels and would remain so for months to come. In early August, he warned that the Taliban were moving beyond their traditional strongholds in southern Afghanistan and beginning to threaten areas in the north and west.

Some believed the Taliban had begun to gain the upper hand, despite the fact that the United States was spending more than $4 billion a month on the war in Afghanistan. Evidence of the rising tide of violence could be seen through the summer of 2009. On June 29, the provincial police chief of Kandahar Province was shot and killed in a shootout between police and an Afghan security squad that had been trained by U.S. forces. On July 6, in Kunduz, in the north, a roadside bomb killed six people, including two Americans. On August 4, Taliban insurgents fired rockets directly into the capital Kabul. In Herat Province, far to the west, on August 6, four more U.S. Marines were killed by a roadside bomb. Several car bombs set off simultaneously killed at least 41 people in Kandahar on August 25. And on December 30, a Jordanian considered to be a trusted informant was allowed into a CIA base in Khost Province, where he detonated a suicide bomb, killing seven CIA officers and his Jordanian handler.

Despite all this, optimists could see some rays of hope in the situation in Afghanistan. First of all, if critics were right, one of the reasons that the war in Iraq had dragged on for so long was simply that the United States did not commit enough forces to the situation to bring peace to that country. Obama decided for Afghanistan, as Bush had decided for Iraq, that if peace were to come, the sheer number of troops from the United States would have to be increased.

The new strategy in Afghanistan did not just rely on more troops. The new U.S. officers in control, like General McChrystal, came with direct experience and background in counterinsurgency. They understood that troops had to be present in neighborhoods and villages and give confidence to the local people that they would be protected against reprisals from the Taliban. Furthermore, the new Obama administration had decided that the problems of Afghanistan and Pakistan were intimately connected and had committed to working toward a regional solution. There were signs that U.S. diplomacy had succeeded in getting the Pakistani government to be more vigorous in eliminating the influence of the Taliban in North-West Frontier Province and Federally Administered Tribal Areas.

Another U.S. strength in Afghanistan was that their effort was supported by a genuine, multinational commitment of troops, led by NATO, and even including some troops from countries outside of NATO. Although troubled by differences in rules of engagement and complicated lines of command, the mere fact that America's war in Afghanistan was shared by many other countries with the same goal of bringing peace and stability to the country was a source of strength and optimism for the United States.

Many Afghans saw the Taliban and al-Qaeda forces as foreign. This was a possible strength for the United States. That is, if Afghans came to understand that the United States only wanted Afghans to run their own country, and if they began to see the Taliban, not as a home-grown movement, but as a group of renegades based over the border in Pakistan, that could work in favor of the United States.

In August 2009, the Afghan people engaged in another national election. Outside observers grew nervous when increased levels of violence threatened the election with some Taliban insurgents pledging to disrupt polling places. Taliban units threatened to bomb a number

THE SURGE IN AFGHANISTAN

In the period of 2007 to 2008, under President Bush, the number of troops in Iraq had been greatly increased, and that increase was known as the surge. When President Obama decided to increase the troop presence in Afghanistan, many editorialists pointed out that he was imitating the surge tactic that apparently had begun to work in Iraq.

After less than a month in office, Obama ordered 17,000 additional troops to Afghanistan. A month later, he ordered 4,000 more troops to serve in Afghanistan as trainers. By late summer 2009, the total of U.S. forces in the country reached about 60,000 and would approach 100,000 in 2010. The troops took on the more aggressive job of policing the southern and eastern provinces where the Taliban forces were the strongest.

As a consequence, American casualty figures began to climb. July and August 2009 saw casualty rates among British and U.S. troops climb to the highest numbers of the whole war. The number of roadside IED detonations increased dramatically, and the Taliban developed a new weapon. The so-called invisible IEDs were made with very little metal, using glass and carbon instead. These new IEDs were almost impossible to detect with traditional mine-detecting gear.

U.S. and NATO military commanders hoped that the increased troop presence would help turn local leaders in the Pashtun regions of the south and east into opponents of the Taliban. Whether their optimism was justified remains to be seen.

On the night of October 29, 2009, President Obama made an unannounced visit to Dover Air Base in Delaware to honor the return of the body of a U.S. soldier killed by a roadside bomb in Afghanistan. *(Department of Defense)*

RICHARD HOLBROOKE AND HIS MISSION

When President Obama appointed Richard Holbrooke as a special envoy to deal with Pakistan and Afghanistan, many observers in Washington and in the region were surprised. Holbrooke had established a tough reputation, and in some quarters he was known as the Bulldozer.

Holbrooke had served under President Clinton as a diplomatic troubleshooter, and he had taken the lead in arranging the Dayton Accords in 1995. That agreement settled an armed conflict that had grown out of ethnic-religious clashes in Bosnia. Holbrooke, for his work in this and other trouble spots, had been nominated seven times for the Nobel Peace Prize.

However, because of tough statements he had made prior to his appointment by President Obama, many thought that Holbrooke would be ready to signal that the United States was going to back away from its support of President Hamid Karzai. He had also been critical of the Bush administration's bombing of opium fields in Afghanistan with defoliants or weed-killers.

In interviews, Holbrooke made it clear that he did not believe that the United States could achieve a traditional victory in Afghanistan. Rather, he hoped that the United States, working with Pakistan and other countries, could stabilize the region.

Holbrooke was known for his experience in talking tough with leaders of corrupt and troubled governments. He faced a daunting challenge in Pakistan, where the central Pakistani government had just concluded compromise agreements with local Taliban leaders in Swat and other regions in the North-West Frontier Province and Federally Administered Tribal Areas.

One part of Holbrooke's mission was to convince the Pakistanis to take a stronger stand against the local Taliban in those regions. Within a few months of his arrival, the Pakistani government did in fact change its position vis-à-vis the Taliban, recognizing that the Taliban could not be trusted to keep to their agreements. The Pakistani army moved into Swat and other regions to exert control. But in January 2010, when Defense Secretary Robert Gates was visiting Pakistan, its army announced that it needed to take a six-month break before undertaking any more military operations.

of polling places, and some remained shut up and unavailable on election day. Several of the numerous candidates for president charged the Karzai regime with stuffing the ballot boxes. When the final results were announced on September 16, it was claimed that Karzai had won 54.6 percent of the vote, thus eliminating the need for a runoff with the runner-up Abdullah Abdullah. The charges of fraud elicited such an international protest that Karzai agreed to a runoff, but on November 1, Abdullah said that he expected yet another fraudulent election and declined to run. With this, Karzai was declared to have won a second term as president. However, the lack of a clear majority diminished domestic and international respect for Karzai, and he faced a future made even more uncertain when he named a cabinet filled with several of the same controversial members.

In the months that followed, Karzai continued to be a somewhat problematic ally, at one point stating that he was prepared to negotiate with the Taliban to form a coalition government. Meanwhile, the first several thousand U.S. troops that were to be part of the "surge" were arriving in Afghanistan, and U.S. forces began to try to put into practice the counterinsurgency strategy formulated by Gen. David Petraeus that since May 2009 had been directed by Lt. Gen. Stanley McChrystal. Then in June 2010, *Rolling Stone* magazine published an article in which the writer quoted General McChrystal and his aides criticizing and mocking various U.S. civilian leaders, including President Obama and Vice President Biden. Although the comments may have reflected tensions between the civilian and military leadership, such public disrespect by a member of the U.S military is absolutely unacceptable conduct. General McChrystal knew this and so submitted his resignation. President Obama had little choice but to accept it, but he appeared to limit the damage by immediately appointing General Petraeus to take command in Afghanistan. No one could have been more prepared to continue the strategy of counterinsurgency that Petraeus himself had designed.

Based on all of the concerns for Afghanistan's future, as U.S. troops went to Afghanistan in greater numbers in 2010, they and their families could only hope for success and that the men and women stationed there would be able to come home safely and in the near future. The sad, but possible, alternative was that the country, as the graveyard of empires, would defeat the U.S.-led effort to convert Afghanistan into a democratic and stable country. The developments of 2010 and later will tell the outcome of this story.

Glossary

Afghan A citizen of Afghanistan.

asymmetrical warfare Warfare conducted by alternate means, such as guerrilla war or terrorist attacks, in which one side has much smaller forces not symmetrical in strength with the other side but nevertheless presenting challenges conventional forces find difficult to counter.

burqa A full-length garment for women, worn from the top of the head to the shoes, completely concealing the body. A small screen in the face mask allows the wearer to see out. This traditional garment was worn in some rural areas of Afghanistan, but the Taliban required that all Afghan women wear it in the areas they controlled from 1993 to 2001.

casus belli From the Latin for "occasion of war," an event or action that justifies war.

coup Short form of coup d'état, meaning a violent overthrow of a government by a small group

Deobandi Islamic sect established in India in 1867 and strong in Pakistan, advocating rejection of Western ideas and forcible spread of Islam.

drone A pilotless remote-controlled aircraft such as the Predator.

Durand Line The boundary established in 1893 in the Pashtun tribal areas between Pakistan and Afghanistan. Named after Sir Mortimer Durand, the British foreign secretary who led the negotiations, it has become a source of controversy between the countries.

fatwa An edict or religious proclamation by a Muslim claiming some authority. It can include a declaration of jihad.

Humvee A light, all-terrain vehicle, larger and more rugged than the traditional jeep. Its name comes from HMMWV, which stands for high-mobility multipurpose wheeled vehicle.

ISAF (International Security Assistance Force) The international forces, including those of NATO, that have assisted U.S. forces in attempting to bring security and peace to Afghanistan.

Islamic Jihad   Organization set up by Ayman al-Zawahiri, holding for an Islamic revival, end of national states, and establishment of worldwide Muslim community.

jahiliyya   The pagan state of the world that existed before the prophet Mohammed; Sayyid Qutb, the Muslim Brotherhood intellectual, claimed all modern life was in a state of jahiliyya.

jihad   The Arabic word for "struggle" or "effort." In the Quran it refers to both a holy war against infidels (the little jihad) and the internal striving by a Muslim to attain perfection in all matters (the great jihad).

Khalq   The more radical faction of the People's Democratic Party of Afghanistan.

Lashkars   Traditional tribal militias in Afghanistan.

LCSFA (Limited Contingent of Soviet Forces in Afghanistan)   The official name for the Soviet military troops in Afghanistan in the period from 1979 to 1989.

loya jirga   A convened assembly of tribal and local leaders in Afghanistan, not held on any particular schedule, brought together to deal with major constitutional and regime-change questions.

madrassa   A Muslim school headed by religious leaders. Most commonly associated with the schools held in Pakistan for refugee boys from Afghanistan but also referring to any religious school, for boys or for girls.

mujahideen   Literally "holy warriors." The name for many different guerrilla armies that opposed the Soviet occupation of Afghanistan.

Muslim Brotherhood (Society of the Muslim Brothers)   Egyptian movement stressing the need for an Islamic revival, establishment of sharia in Egypt, and overthrow of the current moderate government.

NATO (North Atlantic Treaty Organization)   A mutual defense organization of European countries and the United States, originally formed in 1949 to offset possible Soviet expansion into western Europe.

Northern Alliance   The term for a loose coalition of mujahideen forces that resisted the Taliban and were largely responsible for their overthrow in 2001 and 2002.

North-West Frontier Province   One of the four provinces of Pakistan, bordering Afghanistan and largely populated by Pashtun people.

Parcham   Gradualist faction of the People's Democratic Party of Afghanistan, supported by the Soviet Union.

Pashtun   The largest ethnic group in Afghanistan, representing about 40 percent of the population. Also numerous in Baluchistan and the North-West Frontier Province of Pakistan.

Pashtunistan   The concept of a united Pashtun ethnic state, incorporating Pashtun provinces of Afghanistan and Pashtun areas in Pakistan's North-West Frontier Province and Baluchistan. To create such a state would require the abandonment of the Durand Line and the loss of territory by Pakistan and Afghanistan.

Pashtunwali   The set of Pashtun values and social practices, including some that violate precepts in the Quran. The Pashtunwali code of hospitality requires hosts to protect guests from arrest by authorities even if they are fugitive criminals or rebels.

PRTs (Provisional Reconstruction Teams)   The military teams assigned by ISAF to different regions within Afghanistan, each under the command of an officer from either the United States, Britain, or one of the ISAF countries. The PRTs engage in reconstruction efforts at the local and provincial level.

PVSV   Under the Taliban regime in Afghanistan, the Ministry for the Promotion of Virtue and Suppression of Vice; religious police.

al-Qaeda   Literally meaning "the base" in Arabic. An Islamist movement calling for global jihad; espouses the goal of establishing a new caliphate. Responsible for attacks on the United States and other countries, including the 9/11 attacks, bombs at U.S. embassies, and bomb attacks in London and Madrid.

Quran   The holy book of the Muslim religion, consisting of the collected revelations reported by the prophet Muhammed.

sharia   The code of conduct of Muslims. In some Muslim countries, it has become the basis of civil and criminal law. The interpretation of sharia varies considerably from one Muslim country to another and even within countries.

Shia   One of the two major branches of the Muslim religion, whose members tend to closely rely on the advice of religious leaders in matters of political, social, and moral concerns. The Shia and Sunni disagree over questions of the legitimate successors to Mohammed and over matters of adherence to sharia.

Sunni   One of the two major branches of the Muslim religion. Usually, the Sunni are less strict in adherence to sharia than are Shia.

Tajik   The people and language of Tajikistan, one of the former Soviet republics, bordering Afghanistan on the north. A small minority of Tajiks live within Afghanistan.

Taliban   Literally "students." A movement based on graduates of religious schools or madrassas in Pakistan, who established a strict, fundamentalist regime in Afghanistan in 1993. They took power in Kabul in 1996. The regime provided a haven for Osama bin Laden and members of the al-Qaeda organization in the period from 1996 to 2001.

UN (United Nations)   The world organization for peace, social, and cultural affairs, established in 1945. Decisions of the 15-member Security Council are expected to be upheld by all members.

Uzbek   The people and language of Uzbekistan, one of the former Soviet Republics, bordering Afghanistan on the north. A small minority of Uzbek people live within Afghanistan. Many of the troops of the Northern Alliance were Uzbek.

Further Reading

NONFICTION

Carlisle, Rodney. *Iraq War*. Rev. ed. New York: Facts On File, 2010.

———. *Persian Gulf War*. New York: Facts On File, 2003.

Chayes, Sarah. *The Punishment of Virtue*. New York: Penguin, 2006.

Coll, Steve. *Ghost Wars*. New York: Penguin, 2004.

Darack, Ed. *Victory Point: Operations Red Wings and Whalers—The Marine Corps' Battle for Freedom in Afghanistan*. New York: Berkley, 2009.

Griffin, Michael. *Reaping the Whirlwind: Afghanistan, Al Qa'ida and the Holy War*. Sterling, Va.: Pluto, 2003.

Jalali, Ali A. *Afghanistan Guerrilla Warfare: In the Words of the Mujahideen Fighters*. Osceola, Wisc.: Zenith, 2002.

———. *The Other Side of the Mountain: Mujahideen Tactics in the Soviet Afghan War*. Washington, D.C.: United States Marine Corps, 1995.

Kean, Thomas, and Lee H. Hamilton. *The 9/11 Commission Report: Final Report of the National Commission on Terrorist Attacks on the United States*. Washington, D.C.: Government Printing Office, 2005. Available online. URL: http://www.9-11commission.gov/report/911Report.pdf. Accessed May 3, 2010.

Mehta, Sunita. *Women for Afghan Women*. New York: Palgrave, 2002.

Newell, Nancy Peabody, and Richard S. Newell. *The Struggle for Afghanistan*. Ithaca, N.Y.: Cornell University Press, 1981.

Rashid, Ahmed. *Taliban: Militant Islam, Oil and Fundamentalism in Central Asia*. New Haven, Conn.: Yale University Press, 2000.

Rotberg, Robert, ed. *Building a New Afghanistan*. Washington, D.C.: Brookings Institution Press, 2007.

Roy, Oliver. *Afghanistan: From Holy War to Civil War*. Princeton, N.J.: Darwin, 1995.

Scheuer, Michael. *Through Our Enemies' Eyes: Osama bin Laden, Radical Islam, and the Future of America*. Washington, D.C.: Potomac, 2006.

Stanton, Doug. *Horse Soldiers: The Extraordinary Story of a Band of U.S. Soldiers Who Rode to Victory in Afghanistan*. New York: Scribner's, 2009.

Urban, Mark. *War in Afghanistan*. New York: St. Martin's Press, 1988.

Wright, Lawrence. *The Looming Tower: Al-Qaeda and the Road to 9/11*. New York: Knopf, 2006.

FICTION AND MEMOIR

Hosseini, Khaled. *The Kite Runner.* New York: Riverhead, 2003.
———. *A Thousand Splendid Suns.* New York: Riverhead, 2007.
Mortenson, Greg. *Three Cups of Tea: One Man's Mission to Promote Peace . . . One School at a Time.* New York: Penguin, 2007.
Seierstad, Asne. *The Bookseller of Kabul.* Boston: Backbay, 2004.

WEB SITES

Afghanistan Jurist. URL: http://jurist.law.pitt.edu/world/afghanistan.htm.
Afghanistan Reports and Analysis. URL: http://afghanistan-analyst.org.
The Long War Journal. URL: http://www.longwarjournal.org/archives.
Operation Enduring Freedom. URL: http://www.globalsecurity.org.
UN Mission in Afghanistan. URL: http://unama.unmissions.org.
U.S. Army in Afghanistan: Operation Enduring Freedom. URL: http://www.history.army.mil.
U.S. Department of State, Afghanistan Country Report. URL: http://www.state.gov.

DVDS

Charlie Wilson's War
Flight 93

Index

Page numbers in *italic* indicate a photograph. Page numbers followed by *c* indicate chronology entries. Page numbers followed by *m* indicate maps. Page numbers followed by *g* indicate glossary entries. Page numbers in **boldface** indicate box features.

A

Abdel-Rahman, Omar **72**
Abdullah, Abdullah 159
Academy Awards (1999) **67**
act of war **76–77, 122**
Aden, Yemen **74**
adultery 65
Afghan army 27–28, 101, *112, 130,* 132, 145
Afghan Constitutional Commission 93
Afghan Interim Authority 92
Afghanistan *2m, 134m*
  bin Laden's arrival in 44
  cabinet members **110–111,** *111*
  chronology (1919–1992) **20**
  chronology (1989–2001) **55**
  ethnolinguistic groups *14m,* **15**
  history 9–22
  independence (1919) 11–12, 20*c*
  Iraq v. **117,** 154–155
  neighboring countries' policies **151**
  Pakistan and 123–131
  Soviet invasion 16–18, 20*c,* 23–36, *26m*
  Soviet withdrawal from 18, 35–36, 55*c*
  topographical map *134m*
Afghanistan Civil War (1990s) 21–22, 47–48, *51m,* 51–54, 55*c*
Afghanistan Military Forces (AMF) *133*
Afghanistan National Auxiliary Police *153*

Afghanistan National Liberation Front (ANLF)—Jebh-e-Nejat-i-Melli **18–19,** 104
Afghanistan War 79–90
Afghan Mellat (Afghan Social Democratic Party) **108**
Afghans (term) 160*g*
Afghan Transitional Administration x, **105**
Afghan Wars (1839–42/1878–1880) 10
AFPAK policy 131
Africa 23
African U.S. embassy attacks 45, **46,** 73
agriculture xi, 111–112
Ahmadinejad, Mahmoud **151**
air base 82
aircraft 68
Air Force, U.S. *99,* **142**
air strikes 131
air support **94,** 140
AK-47 assault rifles 133, 140
Albania **99**
Albright, Madeleine 66, 67
Alexander III the Great (king of Macedonia) 9
Allah **13**
All-India Muslim League **125**
all-terrain vehicles *83*
Amanullah (king of Afghanistan) 12
ambushes 33
American Flight 11 68
American Flight 75 68, 71
Amerine, Jason 85–86
Amin, Hafizullah 16, 20*c,* 24, **24,** 27, **28**
ammunition **31**
Amnesty International 61–62
Anaconda. *See* Operation Anaconda
Anan, Kofi 59
Anderson, Rafaelina 4